GOING
DOWNHILL FAST
CLEEVES PALMER

Rodney,

thank you so much for looking after us (at) Little Wych for so many years — you are brilliant.

As a non-skier, treat this as a cure for occasional insomnia.

Memories of an Amateur Ski Racer

Yours ever

Cleeves

1

I propose to execute a stop-christiania to the right.

Contents

Achtung! - I am not certain which way I am turning.

This book is dedicated to the memory of my parents Tony and Nora Palmer, without whose love, support and encouragement I would never have discovered the joy of skiing; to the wonderful people of Mürren; and to my ski friends who have left us far too soon but live on in my memory of happy days shared in the mountains - Zannah Stephen, Bill Manson, Peter Barnes, Pat Reeves, Lucy Hulse and Olivia Byrom.

Huge thanks to 'Dwina for all her support and for tolerating my hours on ski business; to her and Ivan Wagner for reading; to Victoria Wright for proof reading; to Paul Eustice for his design expertise and to Adam Ruck for his editorial help. Looking back on my 11 years at boarding school, I must thank the one master at Canford who supported and encouraged my love of skiing: Peter Lewis, a great sportsman and a kind man.

If you have enjoyed this book, please make a donation to British Ski & Snowboard (Charity Number 1167331) www.bssnf.uk. By doing so, you will be directly contributing to the future success of British snowsports athletes.

Going Downhill Fast - Memories of an Amateur Ski Racer
Copyright Cleeves Palmer 2018
Design: PED (Paul Eustice Design)
Printed by Pensord Press

I am about to fall.

Foreword

This is a memoir of a convivial and entertaining skiing life spent in the company of some of the great personalities in Alpine skiing, the Kandahar and Mürren, the birthplace of British ski racing. I am one of the lucky ones whose skiing days have been all the more competitive, rewarding and amusing for being spent in the company of Cleeves Palmer.

In a speech at the Kandahar's 90th birthday dinner in January 2014, I said we should not forget that the Club was not always such a happy and inclusive place. There was a period in the 1970/80s when Peter Lunn felt that its future was in doubt. The importance therefore of certain Kandahar members in shaping the Club's recent history cannot be over-emphasised.

The revival was led by John Boyagis who came in as Chairman and set the Kandahar on a new course as an active amateur racing club. Four men in particular made sure John's vision bore fruit: Ted Varley, Jimmy Riddell, Beat Hodler and Cleeves Palmer. Without their efforts the Club might well have disintegrated.

Cleeves came to the fore as Club Captain in the 1990s as John and the others stepped back. He led by example, never missing an Inferno and carrying off an impressive haul of Club trophies including best British skier in 1997 and winner of the 35 - 49 age category seven times. He is in sight of his third 'Diamond Devil' award, when most Ks would be proud of one.

Attention! I have fallen.

Nick Morgan in the 2018 Inferno. Photo: Beatrice Gertsch

Away from his beloved Inferno, the Amateur Inter-Club Championship is Cleeves's personal creation. His greatest legacy is the spirit of a club that helps and encourages people to race and makes racing available for all who wish to compete. Thanks largely to Cleeves, the Kandahar is again firmly established as one of the world's most active and influential ski racing clubs.

Nick Morgan (Chairman, Kandahar Ski Club, 2011 - 16)

Winner of the Humphreys Cup (Kandahar Inferno Combination) 2007. Photo: Toby Carless

Introduction

In deciding to write this short account of my skiing life - so far - I have been encouraged by the ski historian John Collard and inspired by Sir Winston Churchill, who wrote that "words are the only things that last forever." I also have masses of photos of family and friends to share .... so here goes!

One's greatest loves in life are, or ought to be, for other people. In my case it was for my parents: as a child, without their love and support I would never have started skiing, discovered the thrill of racing or the fantastic pleasure of skiing in deep powder snow. And without skiing, I would have never made the hundreds of friends that I have during my times in the mountains. From the age of 31 it was for my wife Edwina and later for our children Sophie and Mark as well.

As a child I loved playing many sports but my ability on the playing field was somewhere between poor and average. I would have loved to represent my schools in the first team for everything but as it turned out I was never in the first team for anything, apart from Real Tennis. I have been a late developer in co-ordination, determination, competitiveness, fitness and ability. In mid-life, I became average to good at most sports, compared to my own age group. In my 57th year I am pleased that I am yet to become an embarrassment on either the squash or tennis court and I still love playing cricket. It is the last team game that I play, and I play it with good friends.

My mother, Nora Palmer   *My father, Tony Palmer*

But this book is about skiing. My first taste of it was in 1971, and my father generously gave my 8-year-old self the choice of where we should go. Not a wide choice, admittedly: he said it could be Mürren or Villars. Knowing nothing of either resort, I decided that if I chose the former, I would meet our Swiss cousins, so Mürren it was. I eventually skied for a day in Villars with 'Dwina in January 2015. It was lovely to ski where my parents had taken my sisters Anne and Susan and my brother John more than 50 years earlier but, looking back on my decision .... *je ne regrette rien.*

Cleever

Before I was born

In 1930 my grandfather's first cousin Eveline Palmer married an intelligent, shy and entrepreneurial Swiss whom she had met and fallen for in St Moritz. His name was Walter Amstutz. Walter was born in Brienzwiler in 1902 but spent his childhood in Mürren, where the Amstutz family owned the Hotel Alpina. When Walter was eleven, his father slipped and fell off the Mürren cliff just below the hotel. There is no doubt that this terrible loss was the spur to a life of many remarkable achievements.

Walter was determined to educate himself. After skiing down to school in Lauterbrunnen every winter's morning he would climb the steps beside the funicular to Grütschalp each evening and skate up the path back to Mürren. He finished his education by reading Geology, Art, Law and Economics at Bern University and achieved a Doctorate in Economics in 1928 (magna cum laude).

Arnold Lunn was an inspiration and a mentor to him and as the years passed they became close friends, climbing together among the high Alpine peaks of the Bernese

Walter Amstutz in action

Walter Amstutz in the first Anglo-Swiss Slalom, 1925

Arnold Lunn at the Eigerjoch on the first ski ascent of the Eiger, 1924; photo taken by Walter Amstutz

Arnold Lunn's skiing was permanently impaired after a climbing accident left him with one leg shorter than the other

Oberland and working together to promote the new sport of Alpine skiing. The two met in 1916. Walter was 14 and spoke poor English, Arnold was 28 and his knowledge of German was no better. Walter was a bright young man, a great skier and alpinist. Arnold was a visionary with a brilliant brain and wide-ranging interests. They became kindred spirits probably because in many ways they were opposites. Walter would develop into a canny businessman but remained the introvert, keeping his infectious laughter for those he knew well. Arnold was an extrovert intellectual: a dominant personality who spoke and wrote with equal brilliance but had little interest in money.

Arnold Lunn wrote that 1924 made a greater contribution to skiing history than the centuries before or the decades since. On 30th January of that year, at an evening meeting in Mürren, ten British skiers including Mr and Mrs Arnold Lunn founded the Kandahar Ski Club. It was the first ski club dedicated to racing, and it was founded half way through the first Winter Olympic Games which were being held in Chamonix with jumping and cross-country the only skiing disciplines. On 5th February, the International Skiing Commission changed its name to the Fédération Internationale de Ski (FIS), which remains the sport's governing body.

One of the first actions of the new club was to challenge the British skiers of nearby Wengen to a race in both Downhill and Slalom. Wengen turned down this first challenge, but accepted the following year and, after losing heavily, founded its own club, the Downhill Only (DHO), to avenge the defeat. A friendly rivalry was born, and it continues to this day.

Between the foundation of these two essentially British clubs, Walter Amstutz and two Swiss university friends, Hermann (Manz) Gurtner and Willy Richardet, founded a Swiss club, Schweizerische Akademische Skiclub (SAS) on 26th November 1924. The SAS, begotten in Mürren, was founded in Bern.

These crucial developments in the birth of international ski racing might not have been possible but for a spike of rock no more than 1 inch in height that saved the lives of both Arnold and Walter on their ground-breaking first ski descent of the Eiger, on 18th May 1924.

Skiing tied together, one pulled the other over and they tumbled down a steep slope until the small piece of rock intervened, snagging the rope to arrest their fall just above a 1000-ft precipice. It was truly a moment when the future of Alpine ski racing was hung in the balance. Walter talked to me about this narrow escape and quite a few others, but this was surely the narrowest.

On the same day he confided to Arnold that he planned to found the SAS in the autumn, as a Swiss partner for the Kandahar in its campaign for the recognition of Alpine ski racing. Due to the friendship between Walter and Arnold, the SAS and Kandahar became sister clubs, and this is another close relationship that continues to flourish.

Kandahar Ski Club

Swiss Academic Ski Club

Roberts of Kandahar

The Kandahar Ski Club's declared purpose was to raise the standard of British skiing by encouraging participation in Alpine ski racing. Why was the club called Kandahar?

The explanation goes back to a ski race organised at the Swiss resort of Montana for the clients of Arnold Lunn's father's travel company* in 1911, for a trophy to be presented by one of the most famous men of the era. Field Marshal Lord Roberts of Kandahar (1832 - 1914), known to the nation as Bobs, had won the Victoria Cross as a young man and had risen to command the British army. He took his title - 'of Kandahar' - from a great victory in Afghanistan in 1880. In later life he visited Montana in summer, but never skied. The Downhill race for the Roberts of Kandahar trophy became a prestigious annual fixture in Mürren, and the skiers decided to name their new racing club after it.

The centenary of the first Roberts of Kandahar race was celebrated in Montana in 2011, the cup being prominently displayed. A small party of Ks - as Kandahar members call themselves - descended on Crans Montana over the weekend of January 6th - 9th, and James Hopkinson-Woolley, the great great nephew of the inaugural winner, was one of them. An enormous commemorative stone was unveiled in the middle of the resort, where Crans and Montana meet.

*Henry Lunn had founded co-operative educational tours for predominantly British church leaders in Grindelwald between 1892 and 1896. In 1902 he had organised religious/health winter holidays to both Adelboden and Wengen. In 1905 he formed the Public Schools Alpine Sports Club, which made way for Alpine Sports Ltd. (1908), to be followed by Sir Henry Lunn Travel and Lunn Poly which ceased trading in 2005.

Racers before the start of the first Roberts of Kandahar

Four of the finishers. Cecil Hopkinson 2nd from right

Roberts of Kandahar Cup

Lord Roberts of Kandahar VC, KG, GCB, OM, GCSI, GCIE, KStl, VD, PC; by Frank Skipworth, after Singer Sargent

James Hopkinson-Woolley with Kandahar flag-bearer Susie Berry at the Roberts of Kandahar centenary in Crans-Montana; and (right) racing at the 2015 AICC

(Left) Skiing in 1908, by Alan d'Egville

Ivan Wagner of the SAS and Kandahar asked Adam Ruck to write about the event for the SAS's quadrennial yearbook Der Schneehase. I am grateful to both for permission to reprint a shortened version of the article here.

The first Roberts of Kandahar race (January 7, 1911)

When ten British skiers set off from the Wildstrubel Hut at 10 o'clock on a January morning in 1911, and raced down to Montana for a trophy to be presented by an old soldier called Lord Roberts of Kandahar, none can have foreseen the historic significance of their adventure. But Kandahar would become a key brand name in the development of Alpine ski racing, Crans Montana would cherish its place in history, and the route taken by the early racers would become a spectacularly scenic piste enjoyed by thousands of recreational skiers every fine day of the winter season.

The facts of the race are well known, thanks to Sir Henry Lunn's son Arnold, who set the course and was probably responsible for the account which appeared in The Times. Ten members of Sir Henry's Public Schools Alpine Sports Club climbed from Montana to the Wildstrubel Hut on January 6th 1911, and raced back down the next morning, 19 year old Cecil Hopkinson winning in 61 minutes, over an 11.5km course with a drop of around 1500 vertical metres.

A full century later, on a mild January morning, the ski club that took its name from the Roberts of Kandahar race proudly carried its banner and the trophy through the streets of Montana to the new memorial's 'symbolic' location, mid-way between Crans and Montana and close to the site of their first ski lift.

The great and the good of the Haut Plateau turned out in force, including Crans Montana's 'three musketeers' from the 1950s: Andre Bonvin - winner of the

Arlberg Kandahar downhill at St Anton in 1953 - Rene Rey, and Bouby Rombaldi. Flags were raised, and a guard of honour from Chermignon came decked out in colourful uniforms perhaps more reminiscent of the Napoleonic era than the countdown to the First World War.

"You are standing on a high mountain preparing to take part in one of the greatest races in history," declared M Marius Robyr, chairman of Crans Montana's World Championship Organising Committee and mastermind of the day's celebrations. "Two minutes to go - timing brought to you by Hublot!"

Kandahar heads nodded in approval. Henry and Arnold Lunn were visionaries, and their vision was the happy marriage of sport and business, hand in sponsored glove. Indeed that fruitful partnership was the essence of this celebration. The old saying was repeated, that the British taught the Swiss to look at their mountains, but it might be more accurate to say that Henry Lunn showed how to turn them to profit, with prestigious ski racing events underpinning the success of the mountain resort.

The grenadiers fired their guns in the air on the stroke of ten o'clock, and M Robyr paid eloquent tribute to the Public School pioneers. "C'était vraiment la course des héros," he said; "une épreuve qui, on peut le dire, révolutionna l'histoire mondiale du sport blanc." Curé Gérald Voide invited all present to pray for snow and think of the downhill ski race as a metaphor for Our Lord's descent among us. Whereupon he blessed the newly unveiled memorial rock and sprinkled the onlookers with Holy Water for good measure.

For the Kandahar, Club President Beat Hodler spoke of Arnold Lunn's achievement in '12 golden years' from 1924, when the foundation of the Kandahar and SAS ski clubs marked the start of the campaign for the recognition of Alpine racing, to 1936 when it made its debut at the Winter Olympics.

"But was it really the world's first downhill ski race?" the Kandahar's former President and unofficial historian Andrew Morgan was asked after the ceremony. "It is now!" he replied. As Arnold Lunn knew, the best way to make history is to write it, and erect memorials.

More than a commemoration, the meeting at Montana was a chance for interested skiers from Switzerland and Great Britain to get together, open old maps and photograph albums and ponder unanswered questions. Where was the Palace Hotel? Was the Wildstrubel Hut in the same place in 1911 as it is now? How much has the Plaine Morte glacier changed in one hundred years? Where exactly did the race end? Not all these questions found answers.

For many present, it was also a first opportunity to study a fascinating account of the race unearthed by James Hopkinson-Woolley from the archives of St Paul's school magazine, and written by one of the competitors.

As well as being a marvellously vivid piece of descriptive writing, this account gives a wealth of detail about the race and a precious snapshot of skiing in Switzerland as practised in the early days of the sport: a world of adventure, sporting endeavour and much laughter.

The article is signed CNB and dated February 1911. CNB says he came fifth in the race, and by cross referencing with The Times, we can identify him as Captain Buzzard.

CNB refers to the event as "the first race for the cup presented by Lord Roberts of Kandahar", although anyone who inspects the trophy can observe that its winners go back to 1903, when AW Lawrence took the prize. Be that as it may, CNB describes the 1911 race as "somewhat of a novelty, at least for English people."

"Ski races are held in the neighbourhood of all Swiss winter resorts," he continues, "but they generally consist of an hour or two's climb and a rapid descent on the slopes near the hotels." So the novelty of the 1911 race lay in its long-distance nature, and, perhaps, the fact that the uphill leg of the expedition was not part of the race.

To describe the novelty race as a pure downhill, however, is not quite accurate since the competitors spent the first half of it climbing up to and across the Plaine Morte glacier. One competitor had the misfortune to fall in a crevasse. Whether this was Arnold Lunn's younger brother Brian, who finished 8th with a broken collar bone, is not known.

Had the intention been to stage a 'pure' downhill race, the skiers could have regrouped at the pass after crossing the glacier, and started from there. But they did not, because 'downhill' had not yet crystallised as an objective. "The long-distance ski race is intended to encourage ski mountaineering," states CNB.

Here we may discern the guiding hand of Arnold Lunn, whose first love was mountaineering, and who was on a mission to persuade more of his countrymen to take it up in winter, against the prevailing view in English mountaineering circles that skis should not be used in high Alpine terrain because of the risk of avalanche.

Setting off from the Palace Hotel - now the Clinique Bernoise - on the morning of the 6th with guides and porters, the group took eight hours to reach the Wildstrubel Hut. Deteriorating weather ruled out a leisurely picnic lunch in the sun, and a blizzard greeted them to the Plaine Morte glacier where they were enveloped in swirling clouds of snow and had difficulty following their leader.

By nightfall the temperature in the hut had fallen to minus 20C. After a typical evening's après-ski - story-telling and song, huddled around the fire - all went to bed fully clothed but for their boots, one member of the party applying a top layer of pink pyjamas over breeches, coat and puttees. In the morning they woke to find everything frozen: oranges, wine, bottles of tea and, worst of all, boots.

After thawing their boots for an hour the skiers set off from the hut at 10 o'clock, and CNB makes it clear that this was the start of the race. The gallant trail-breaker, Collins, closely followed by Hopkinson, took half an hour to cross the glacier and reach the pass between the Tubang and Mont Bonvin - leaving 31 minutes for Hopkinson's descent. Half an hour from Plaine Morte to Montana, through untracked snow, would be a good time today. In 1911, it was a remarkable feat of skiing. From the pass, the racers pointed their skis downhill and tackled the slopes familiar to anyone who skis down from Plaine Morte today, although naturally without the assistance of a smooth zigzag piste. CNB writes of "a series of very steep slopes …. In order to negotiate them one must ski down as steeply as possible in one direction then do an Alpine turn and ski in the other direction. A good skier will leave a beautiful track like a series of S's."

Many of the racers were unequal to this challenge, performing "superb somersaults". Cecil Hopkinson, by contrast, "was soon out of view. His turns are marvellous. One can single out his track with ease - skis close together, with scarcely a touch of the stick." Even so, the runner-up finished only five minutes after Hopkinson, closely followed by the next three. The last man down completed the course in one hour and 50 minutes.

For students of the evolution of skiing technique, these remarks are of the greatest interest. What stage had skiing reached by January 1911? Were they stick-riding, telemarking, or by 'Alpine turn' does CNB mean Zdarsky's Austrian method, which Hannes Schneider was just beginning to refine in the Arlberg?

CNB ends his account with comments that shed further light on this aspect: future competitors are advised to familiarise themselves with "very steep awe-inspiring slopes of great altitude. You may be able to do 'Telemarck' turns beautifully on suitable slopes near a hotel, and yet on a longer descent find yourself unequal to the simpler 'S' turns which are a sine qua non in mountaineering."

A combination of different methods was doubtless employed: Z-turns, S-turns, schuss-and-crash. But Cecil Hopkinson was clearly a skier of high class, and a master of the pure christiania. A group photograph of some of the racers shows them with two sticks, not one.

The racers' route down through the woods to Montana is more difficult to pin down with certainty.

Wherever the finish was, Arnold Lunn was waiting a little above it, and Cecil Hopkinson stopped to shake hands with him before completing his victory.

CNB records the express wish of Lord Roberts that future editions of the race would be held at Montana, where he was staying at the time of the outbreak of the South African War (1899). This did not stop the Lunns taking the Roberts of Kandahar to Mürren, where they opened the Palace Hotel in 1912. Racing from the top of the Schilthorn, J Mercer won three times in a row (1912 - 14) and kept the cup. Its replacement was later lost in a fire, so the present cup is the grandchild of that won by Cecil Hopkinson.

Although tipped by Captain Buzzard to defend his title, Cecil Hopkinson did not win the Roberts of Kandahar again. From Cambridge he joined an engineering firm in Newcastle, took a commission with the Royal Engineers on the outbreak of war and, 15 months after suffering a shrapnel wound to the head, died on 9th February 1917, aged 25.

But Cecil Hopkinson lives on in our memory, skimming effortlessly down a pristine snowfield at exhilarating speed, in a glorious adventure. The serpentine track he leaves behind is beautiful; skis close together, with scarcely a touch of the stick.

A worthy downhill champion, indeed, but was he really the first? He is now. However, the Committee of the Public Schools Alpine Sports Club recognised the continuity of the Roberts of Kandahar with an older competition involving cross-country skiing, skating and tobogganing. The names of the winners from 1903 to 1910 - including Arnold Lunn in 1904 - are engraved on the plinth.

After the unveiling ceremony described in Adam's article, a few of us took the lifts up to Plaine Morte where we admired the sublime view, pored over maps in the restaurant and walked up to a belvedere in an attempt to identify the route of the 1911 race.

Initially we wondered how the racers could have skied across the glacier and up to the saddle in such a short time. It was only later that I discovered in the town library that the glacier had ablated (shrunk) by an incredible 71 metres (220 feet) in the intervening century. We then retraced the steps of the original downhillers of 100 years before, following the easy piste after a few shaky off-piste turns. It was an emotional re-enactment, even if snow conditions were disappointing and the Wildstrubel Hut was closed.

The first Roberts of Kandahar was an arduous and exacting adventure, and a landmark in Alpine ski racing. In addition to Captain Buzzard's article, there are excellent accounts in both the British Ski Year Book and Peter Lunn's Guinness Book of Skiing. The race carried on in the years 1912 - 39, usually in Mürren and organised in its later years by the Kandahar. The founders of the Inferno regarded it as a model for the long-distance race they introduced in 1928. An account of the 1931 race, written by a Canadian visitor and first published in a Canadian ski magazine, appears in the 1932 Kandahar Review.

Above: Ivan Wagner (SAS) and me above the Plaine Morte Glacier on the 100th birthday of the first Roberts of Kandahar race

Left: Diamond Devils - Ed Killwick (red jersey), Nigel Fawkes (front left) and me, Inferno 2011. Photo: Nick Morgan

"Finally I saw the famous Roberts of Kandahar race won this year by Peter Lunn, Arnold Lunn's eldest son, at 16 years of age a magnificent skier. If you can picture a "geschmozzle start"; that is all competitors starting at once down a rough mountainside, through brush and trees, over and around huge boulders and every sort of obstacle; a vertical descent of more than 1,000 ft. over approximately a mile and a quarter being won in 3.10 minutes then you know how the British can ski and what courage and skill they attain too! At one point in the course a heavy board fence has had to be erected to prevent competitors shooting over the ledge on to the heads of those below. Strong men quiver with fatigue and strain at the half-way mark in that race!"

The race continued after the War, becoming part of the British Racing Week and the 'Lowlanders' races, which Arnold Lunn introduced for the benefit of ski racers from non-mountainous countries. After these fell into abeyance in the late 1990s the Kandahar decided to present the Roberts cup to members who qualify for the award of a 'Diamond Devil' in the Inferno, Mürren's annual 'people's downhill' which was founded by Kandahar members in 1928 and inspired by the original 1911 race. I have had the good fortune to be presented with the Roberts of Kandahar twice, in 1999 and again in 2011.*

For the 1910/11 season Sir Henry Lunn, as he now was, persuaded the relevant owning parties to run the funicular and train service to Mürren in winter for the first time. The following year he bought the Palace Hotel and moved the Roberts of Kandahar downhill from Montana to Mürren, where the new Allmendhubel funicular offered lift-served skiing, a dangerous concept described by Arnold Lunn as "a descent of 1000 feet without the appropriate service of upward toil." But just around the corner was the Great War, which would claim Cecil Hopkinson and two of my great uncles, Eddie and Leslie Palmer.

---

* Inferno silver (3 points) and bronze (1 point) medals are awarded to racers who finish within 130% or 160% of the fastest time in their age and gender category. Racers who accumulate 20 points in at least twelve Infernos are awarded a Diamond Devil badge.

Due to Arnold Lunn's injuries from an earlier climbing accident, he was unable to serve in the armed forces, so he spent most of the war years in Mürren, writing and managing the Palace, where convalescing British prisoners of war were interned under terms agreed between Switzerland and the hostile powers. Among those who married local girls was the father of my good friend Ted Varley.

Arnold organised ski tests and ski tours for a few of the interned during the war, and in 1921 staged a British National Ski Championship at Wengen, including a downhill ski race for the first time. Fifteen competitors raced from the Lauberhorn mountain above Kleine Scheidegg to a finish just below Salzegg on the slopes above Grindelwald, this race accounting for half the marks in the championship. The other half were for style, awarded by four judges.

Arnold felt that this method of deciding the championship was too subjective: the stopwatch was the way forward. He saw style not as an end in itself, but as a means to an end: the skier with better technique would prevail in the race.

However, he also accepted that some aspects of skiing technique were not tested in a downhill race and developed the idea of a new racing format that would complement the speed, strength and bravery required for a downhill by testing a skier's balance, agility, smoothness and control of the ski, without the need for subjective judging.

He named the new race after a Norwegian style test, the Slalom. This short race course was marked by gates made up of pairs of poles with flags on top, and they were placed strategically in order to test the racer's ability to make sudden turns at speed. The first such race, on 21st January 1922, was set on the slopes above the Hotel Jungfrau in Mürren. The principles of slalom racing have changed little since then: two runs on different courses with the times added together; disqualification if a gate is missed.

Arnold Lunn might not have approved of my dumbing-down influence on his invention. In the late 1980s when I started to organise the Inferno Kandahar Race week, it occurred to me that slalom racing had become highly technical, and many of our members rarely competed in it. We therefore decided that in our Club Slalom and Giant Slalom races only the best run of two would count. Invariably the best skier still won, but many more racers achieved a result. I'm glad to say there have been few complaints.

Slalom was added to the British Championship in 1923 and the Alpine combination, made up of Downhill and Slalom, came in the following year. In January 1925 Walter Amstutz and Arnold Lunn, with the support of their two clubs, founded the world's first team race, the Anglo-Swiss. Arnold's British team lost the inaugural challenge, but for the future he felt that the team to face the SAS should also be a university team and to this end founded the British Universities Ski Club (BUSC). The downhill race in 1925 was set on the Scheidegg slopes above Grindelwald and the Slalom was set in Mürren the following day.

The Anglo-Swiss races are as keenly fought today as they were more than 90 years ago. In 2016 a seniors' trophy was introduced for past generations of racers. This seniors' team trophy was given by me and Ivan Wagner, a close friend and a senior figure within SAS, who in recent years has worked tirelessly as editor of 'Der Schneehase', one of the world's leading ski publications.

Arnold Lunn's place in the history of ski sport is assured. Without his determination, intellect and sheer persistence winter sports would have developed very differently. Lunn, supported and advised by Walter Amstutz, secured the recognition of downhill and slalom racing at a FIS (Federation International de Ski) meeting in Oslo in 1930. The FIS invited the Ski Club of Great Britain - in effect, Arnold Lunn - to stage the FIS downhill at Mürren in 1931.

This was later recognised as the first World Championship in Alpine racing, and in all sport it remains the only World Championship organised by one nation on the soil of another.

After this major breakthrough, Alpine skiing made its Olympic debut at the 1936 Games, held at Garmisch-Partenkirchen under the dark shadow of Nazi Germany. The short period between 1920 and 1936 later became known as the 'Golden Age' of skiing. Some might say it ended earlier, when Great Britain came off the gold standard in 1931. The financial crisis stopped the travel boom in its tracks.

The second World Championship, then known as the European Ski Championship, took place in Cortina d'Ampezzo in 1932, and Rösli Streiff, whom I later came to know well, won the Slalom by eight seconds. More than half a century later I asked her how she had won by such a large margin. "I saw all the other girls telemarking," she replied, "and I thought that if I stem turned I would be so much quicker!"

I organised an impromptu 90th birthday party for Rösli at the Jungfrau Hotel in Mürren in January 1991. Light-hearted, bubbly and always great fun, she had learned to ski in Mürren and finished her skiing days there as well. She made such an impression on my brother John and his wife Lucille, they named their second daughter after her. Rösli died in 1997 aged 96; a great lady, fondly remembered.

In old age Sir Arnold Lunn was asked in a television interview about the campaign for the acceptance of Alpine racing and those early meetings with the FIS. It was an opportunity to repeat one of his favourite anecdotes.

"When I went to the congress to ask for recognition of the British rules for downhill and slalom racing, the President said, 'what would you think if we Norwegians tried to alter the rules of cricket?' I said, I wish to God you would, we might have fewer draws!"

In the three years around the acceptance of these rules by FIS in 1930, 55% of cricket Test Matches around the world were draws, in contrast to the modern era: in 2017 just over 10% of Test Matches were drawn. So the rules did not need altering, by Norwegians or anyone else. I do not wish to digress too far from skiing, but as a firm believer in Test cricket I side with the great West Indian captain Clive Lloyd's view: "Test Match cricket is an examination, 20/20 cricket is an exhibition."

Not every British skier arriving in Mürren was judged to be of a high enough standard to join the Kandahar Ski Club. One element of the entrance examination was to ski a slope known as Lone Tree without putting in a turn. For readers familiar with the lie of the land in Mürren - and I guess most of my readers will be - this is a slope (now off-piste) which leads steeply down from a point about two thirds of the way along the Hog's Back, where a tree once stood, towards the Maulerhubel chairlift. The Lone Tree even had a ski club named after it for a dozen years (1926 - 34), for aspiring Kandahar members who were not quite good (or brave) enough. In the golden age of British skiing, this slope must have been a tough proposition to skiers who had to contend with lace-up boots, skis without edges and no prepared pistes. This little ditty is from the Kandahar Songbook:

'And he who will not take it straight
Down Lone Tree Slope to Menin gate
Why let the poltroon learn to skate
And quit the Kandahar'

Swiss (dark blue) and British (light blue) teams at the Anglo-Swiss, St Moritz, 2015

Viscount Knebworth was the fastest British skier (7th) in the Downhill at the first World Championships, Mürren, 1931

Rösli Streiff, Slalom champion

The Lone Tree was outlived by the Lone Tree Club. Arnold Lunn told the story of its demise in the 1931 K Review:

The Lone Tree Tragedy

Lone Tree, the most famous of Alpine trees, is dead. Lone Tree had a personality which few trees possess. No skier who has taken Lone Tree straight will ever forget the sight of that tree on the first occasion that he pointed his ski down to the unplumbed depths below. Lone Tree wasn't an ash, a pine or a larch. It was a scraggy, leafless skeleton but with austere dignity all its own. I can see it, as I write, pointing a floppy finger down Lone Tree Slope. When, as usually happened, one had thought better of it and - instead of taking it straight - had traversed down towards Menin Gate*, Lone Tree shrugged its shoulders and sniffed as one passed. If, on the other hand, one decided to take it straight, Lone Tree looked non-committal. "Very well, but don't say I didn't warn you," it seemed to say and its branches seemed to sigh with horror as one dived past.

That first straight run! That awful moment when one's ski started moving; the swift acceleration when the ground falls over steeply just beside Lone Tree itself; the effort of one's stomach to remain behind on the slope; the hideous moment as one's ski leap across the traverse tracks; the agony of fear as one's ski quiver at the abrupt change of gradient near the run-out; the superb, godlike, clamorous triumph as one swings to rest.

One February night in 1930, a moonlight party left the summit of the Allmendhubel. A few criminals, whose names shall be withheld, had the intention of playing a practical

---

* Arnold Lunn states clearly that skiing to Menin Gate was not taking Lone Tree straight, it was the cop-out option. The words of ditty should have been 'down Lone Tree Slope to Scara Gate'. This is a puzzle. Perhaps these place names and their exact whereabouts were not quite so well known as we imagine.

joke on Mr. Arnold Lunn, who was known to cherish feelings of very special and religious reverence for Lone Tree.

They had taken with them a tin of petrol, which they poured over the tree, under the impression (a) that a momentary blaze would not damage Lone Tree, and (b) that Mr. Arnold Lunn's cries of agony would be very diverting. (b) was correct, (a) was incorrect.

Ordinary trees might have recovered from a momentary blaze; not so Lone Tree. For years Lone Tree had been accorded the respect due to a great and famous institution; its name had been linked with deeds of daring; the sight of its sagging branches struck terror into the boldest of hearts. The shock proved fatal, Lone Tree never recovered, its heart was broken, it just withered away and died. The tree which had weathered a thousand storms succumbed to the first of the spring gales and collapsed on the slope which had made it famous.

On December 28th 1930 a funeral procession formed up in front of The Palace Hotel. All were wearing sacks, the nearest to sackcloth and ashes that could be found. The procession was led by Mr. A. H. d'Egville, wearing a diminutive bowler hat and a large false nose and trailing an empty petrol can on which the chief mourner beat a funeral tattoo.

As we passed the rink, we suddenly realised the presence of the King of the Belgians. Deggers lost his nerve and fled, bowler hat, false nose and all. Mr. A. Lunn did his best to explain, but it is difficult to be dignified with a large sack flopping about one's body.

The next day the King met Deggers and said with a smile: "I saw you yesterday, but I did not wish to interrupt you because it was clear that you were conducting a very important ceremony".

The funeral procession proceeded in state to Lone Tree Slope, where Arnold Lunn delivered a short funeral address and three loud boos were given for the criminal. The chief criminal, by the way, had wisely left Mürren. He had been warned that feeling was running very high and that the police were not in a position to guarantee adequate protection.

Lone Tree was then conveyed down to Mürren. The last sad ceremonies were enacted in front of The Palace Hotel, where Lone Tree was cut into sections which will be given in future in honour of distinguished services to the Club.

After it was all over, Deggers remarked to the present writer: "You know, it was odd, but in spite of sacks and a false nose, and the general atmosphere of a rag, I felt hideously depressed as we followed Lone Tree down to Mürren."

Deggers was right. The old Tree, lying down the slope in a position of futile helplessness seemed more than human: a proud monarch uprooted and dethroned. As we had followed it down towards Mürren, we felt as if a great landmark, a link with the past, which held so many memories, was on its way to join dead yesterdays.

The next step up from Mürren?

Alan D'Egville, the life and soul of every Kandahar party

EXTRACT FROM BRITISH SKI TEST REGULATIONS (TURNS):

" Candidates whose turns are consistently uncertain or unsteady should not be passed even though they do not fall."

Hannes Schneider. Photo: New England Ski Museum

Alan D'Egville - Deggers - was at the centre of Kandahar life, and he was sorely missed after his death in 1951. A founder member of Kandahar and a fabulous cartoonist, he was responsible for the 'K' badge. At the foundation meeting of the Club, various suggestions were made, but Deggers insisted: a simple K would suffice. When someone protested, "a K has nothing to do with skiing and nobody will know what it stands for", Deggers replied: "well if they ask you, you just say, 'if you want to know what K stands for, you can bloody well find out for yourself.' And they bloody well will find out for themselves."

Deggers was famous for clowning and could turn a tricky situation into hilarity in seconds. His presence in Mürren was a draw for many friends, who would plan their trip to coincide with his time there. He was an Intelligence Officer in both wars and in peacetime wrote and illustrated books about his passions in life, skiing and fly fishing. But he was often, in the words of his obituary, 'flat broke', and could barely pay for essential surgery when illness took hold. My generation never knew him, but a cup was given in his memory, to be awarded to the fastest Kandahar man in the 36 - 49 age group in the Inferno Downhill. I was the proud recipient on more than one occasion.

Arnold Lunn and Hannes Schneider

It was Deggers who with Walter Bernays engineered the first meeting between Arnold Lunn and Hannes Schneider, the dynamic Director of the Arlberg Ski School, in February 1927. It would lead to a lifelong friendship and a partnership that paved the way for international ski racing as we know it today. Either side of the Great War, Schneider developed the revolutionary Arlberg skiing technique and a teaching system for the Arlberg Ski School. He was a magnetic personality with international celebrity status thanks to his starring roles in Arnold Fanck's mountain films, which did so much to spread the popularity of skiing.

Schneider's ski school launched St Anton

The meeting in February 1927 could not have gone better. Arnold set a slalom, gave a small cup to the winner, and the two new friends agreed to establish a series of downhill and slalom races to be called the Arlberg Kandahar (AK). The first races took place on 31st March and 1st April 1928 in St. Anton. Walter Amstutz came 3rd in the slalom and 5th in the downhill.

In 1929 and 1930 the AK races again took place in St. Anton, but in 1931 they came to Mürren, then alternated between the two resorts in the years leading up to World War Two. When the AK was in St. Anton, Hannes was the referee and Arnold set the course; vice versa when the AK was in Mürren.

As Nazi Germany's tentacles tightened their grip on large swathes of Austria, Hannes Schneider was caught up in anti-Jewish fervour. He had Jews for friends, made no secret of his opposition to Nazism and there is no doubt that the Nazis were jealous of his 'prestige and success', as his friend of 25 years Alice Kiaer wrote after his death in 1955.

In the British Year Book of 1936 Arnold Lunn wrote the following:

"In the Arlberg the racers meet not as representatives of nations, but as members of the skiing brotherhood. They race not to prove that one political system or ski school is superior to a rival system or school, but to prove that they are faster downhill than their rivals … Perhaps it is the personality of Hannes which is more responsible than any other single factor for the AK atmosphere. The ten years that have passed since Walter Bernays introduced me to Hannes have only served to deepen my respect and affection for this paladin of skiing. He dominates St Anton, not only by virtue of his success as a teacher and his great record as an active skier, but by force of his engaging personality. His leadership is a leadership of character and there is a granite-like integrity about the man which is unaffected by the vacillations of political fashion."

Hannes Schneider and Arnold Lunn in 1949   **Roger Bushell**

On March 14th 1938 Arnold Lunn received a telephone call in Rome informing him that Hannes Schneider had been arrested and imprisoned by the Nazis in Landeck. He immediately left for St Anton and called a meeting for members of the Kandahar, including the British Captain, Jimmy Palmer-Tomkinson. The meeting decided that the AK should be cancelled for that year.

Releasing Hannes from captivity was a two-stage process that took almost a year. Prime movers in the first phase were Alice Kiaer and a brave German lawyer, Dr. Karl Rösen, whose widow I met several times. Alice and Karl met secretly in Innsbruck, and Karl managed to arrange for Hannes to stay under house arrest in Garmisch. But for their efforts, there is every chance that he would have been taken to a concentration camp. An early supporter of Alpine ski racing, Dr. Rösen had been made an Honorary Member of the Kandahar on a visit to Mürren in 1929.

Various plans were then hatched, to get Hannes and his family out of Germany. In the end one of his former ski instructors, Benno Rybizka, based in the New Hampshire ski resort of North Conway, set the ball rolling by lobbying Harvey Gibson, a successful businessman who was keen to develop North Conway.

Gibson had lent the previous German government several million dollars and, with the Nazis keen to keep these loans open, he had a lever to secure Schneider's release. With his family he crossed the Atlantic on the Queen Mary and arrived in North Conway in February 1939. Gibson and Hannes became great friends and the family was made to feel at home, but within six months Ludwina Schneider fell ill and died, aged only 49. She and her family had been persecuted by the Nazis in St Anton, although it was the town of her birth.

Hannes Schneider never returned to live in his beloved Austria, but he did make annual visits to hunt in the mountains above his childhood home. He died in the United States in 1955 at the comparatively young age of 64.

World War Two claimed the lives of many great skiers and the Kandahar Ski Club lost 40 members, including Squadron Leader Roger Bushell, the architect of 'The Great Escape' (played by Richard Attenborough in the film), who was murdered by the Gestapo.

After the War the AK was revived, with other venues invited to host the Championship - Chamonix in 1948, Sestriere in 1951 and Garmisch in 1954. This helped the races grow in stature and attract the finest racers of the day. Until the World Cup was launched in 1967 the AK was the most prestigious Alpine combination ski racing event in the world. Collaboration with the Arlberg made Kandahar a global skiing brand and added to the prestige of the Kandahar Ski Club. Mürren hosted the AK for the last time in 1971.

In 1929, a year after his participation in the second AK, Walter Amstutz moved to St Moritz to become the resort's first Kurdirektor. There he met my cousin Eveline

Above: the Amstutz Spring

Below: Walter Amstutz came to our wedding - his last visit to England

St Moritz still uses the sun logo created by Walter Amstutz

Palmer; they married a year later. Walter introduced St Moritz's iconic sun motif, the Engadine being a sunny corner of Switzerland boasting 300 annual days of sunshine. He also inaugurated the 'flying kilometre' speed skiing contest, which much later - at Albertville in 1992 - became a test event at the Winter Olympics. Perhaps the greatest of Walter's skiing initiatives was the invention of the Amstutz Spring in 1930 - the first step towards a fixed-heel binding.

Walter's business career was long and successful. Away from skiing, in 1938 he co-founded Amstutz and Herdeg, an advertising agency that later became a publishing company. In 1963 he founded De Clivo Press, translating books from English to German (and vice versa) - works by Winston Churchill, George Bernard Shaw and George Orwell as well as many titles on art, travel, mountaineering and skiing. 'Who's Who in Graphic Art' first published in 1962, was re-published in 1982 with fellow SAS member Ivan Wagner contributing to the Czech section.

Walter Amstutz remained active in business into his nineties and in his 82nd year was honoured for his services to Anglo-Swiss relations; he was the only Swiss OBE at the time. Bearing in mind his adventures as an alpinist over 70 years, climbing more than 800 worldwide peaks including 50 of the 82 Alpine peaks above 4000m, many first ascents and descents, with more than a few close scrapes .... he was fortunate to enjoy a long life.

He often talked about his seven lives and how lucky he had been on many occasions in the high Alps, and beyond. Walter was in his 80s, with his Mürren climbing companion Franz Sonderegger in the Southern Alps of New Zealand, when they were stuck in a blizzard for four days at high altitude on Mount Cook ....

The inscription on Walter's chalet in Mürren sums up his adventurous spirit. Translated from German, it reads: "Happiness shall always be found by those who dare and persevere. Wanderer, do not turn round. March on and have no fear."

Sir Arnold Lunn in 1970

The close friendship between Lunn and Amstutz lasted until Lunn's death in 1974 at the age of 88. Five years later Walter spoke about his friend's life in a superb address for the Arnold Lunn Memorial Lecture at the Ski Club of Great Britain. He included this prayer which was discovered in one of Lunn's prayer books after his death.

"Let me give thanks, dear Lord
In the frailty of age
For the beloved mountains of my youth,
For the challenge of rock
And for the joy of skiing.
For the friends with whom I climbed and skied,
And above all, dear Lord,
For those moments of revelation
When the temporal beauty of the mountains
Reinforces my faith in the Eternal beauty
Which is not subject to decay."

*With my father on my
first skiing holiday in
Mürren, 1971*

*The 3rd, 4th and 5th generations of the von Allmen-Stähli family of the
Hotel Eiger in Mürren*

The Palace Hotel Ballroom as it is today

Boyhood Friends
and Heroes

I have been blessed with a good memory and my first visit to Switzerland remains clear in my mind, from the moment we got off the train at the wrong Interlaken station, as thousands have done before and since. In Lauterbrunnen we discovered that due to some incident the funicular from the valley floor to Grütschalp was not running and we had to spend the night at the Silberhorn Hotel. Before being sent to bed I looked up at Wengen and was convinced it was a collection of bright stars in the clear alpine sky.

The early winter of 1971/2 was cold, sunny and short of snow. We stayed at the Palace, not yet having discovered the delights of the Hotel Eiger, which four generations of the von Allmen/Stähli family have built up and run wonderfully well, entertaining us all with delicious food in the Eiger Stübli and long nights of dancing in the Tächi Bar.

The Palace was a charmingly Edwardian place in those days. I remember its beautiful dining room with a trio playing music at lunch time and a magnificent ball room where we celebrated New Year's Eve. It was the first time I had been allowed to see the New Year in.

My first skiing experience was a struggle. In lace-up boots and on long skis with cable bindings, I trudged for long hours around the lower nursery slope near the Stäger Stübli with Hilde, while my father and brother skied with Gottlieb Jaun on the more challenging nursery slopes behind the Jungfrau Hotel. My mother had retired from

John Boyagis, British Slalom Champion, 1950

Beautiful Mürren

skiing and was content to watch from the sidelines.

The four of us spent time with our Swiss cousins Eveline and Walter Amstutz and their close friends Ted and Aliki Varley whose children Chloë and Royston had both represented Great Britain at skiing. After the early death of my father fifteen years later, Ted became my skiing mentor, advising, supporting and encouraging me in Mürren, as John Boyagis did on the Kandahar Board of Directors. John was a strong and on occasions direct leader who became a good friend as the years passed. He deserves as much credit as anyone for the revival in Kandahar fortunes after a spell in the doldrums, by shifting the Club's focus back to driving forward amateur ski racing.

Ted and Aliki's son Royston was soon to become Britain's highest placed downhill racer at the 1972 Winter Olympics in Sapporo. More famously - in Kandahar circles, at least – in 1970 he was the last British winner of the Inferno, a great achievement that is hard to see being repeated. Royston carried on racing the Inferno until the

Lots to say, aged 2 (1964). Photo: W.H. Cumming of Weymouth

late 1990s, by which time we had raced in more than ten Infernos together. Of all the great racers that Mürren has produced, the one I have come to know best is my neighbour Kurt Huggler who skied for Switzerland in the early days of the World Cup and came second in the 33rd Arlberg Kandahar downhill, at Chamonix in 1968.

I was extremely close to both my parents and as their youngest child I was undoubtedly spoilt. I loved my childhood but being so much younger than my brother, and with boarding school friends scattered far and wide, I was often lonely in the holidays.

Losing my father while I was still growing up left a void in my life - the only positive is that it forces you to grow up quickly. Meeting 'Dwina put my loss in perspective: in the same year as my father's death she had lost her father and brother in a car crash in France. Our children Sophie and Mark knew neither of their grandfathers.

I am not sure why skiing and the Alps had such a magnetic fascination for me. Could my love of snow have its origins in the hard winter of 1962/63 when I spent many hours looking at it from my pram? More likely, it was due to my struggles in other sports. In skiing I soon realised that I had good natural balance.

My mother and father took me skiing every year in the 1970s and I was lucky with all my ski instructors - Caspar in Wengen, Robert Willen in Adelboden, Chris Graf and Roland Blaesi in Lenzerheide. The name of my instructor in Arosa eludes me, probably because I contracted flu during the holiday and then crashed into a river during a race. It was great to return to this beautiful resort 39 years later, on an off-piste day with Louis Tucker in spring 2015.

I was excited when my father told me that he planned to buy an apartment in our beloved Mürren. We acquired our base there in 1977, in time for a run of great winters that lasted through to the mid-1980s, with abundant snowfalls and superb skiing conditions in Mürren. I made good friends there during my late teens and did a lot of skiing with a pretty Swiss girl named Marianne.

My brother John and I were invited to join the Kandahar on the same day in the spring of 1982. Our proposer was the late John Palmer (no relation), a strong, brave skier whose death in a skiing accident the following year was a terrible blow. John was skiing at Grindelwald at the time, supporting our Club's team in the annual Pentathlon organised by the Swiss Academic Ski Club (SAS). His daughter Melanie was a splendid Editor for the Kandahar, producing 25 excellent Reviews from 1990.

The SAS Pentathlon grew out of a Scottish event that included cross-country running and shooting; the five elements of the SAS version are giant slalom, ski jumping, curling, cross-country skiing and swimming. The SAS has earned a reputation for typical Swiss efficiency in the organisation of this great event, and they have always been the most considerate and charming of hosts. Down the years the mainstays of the event have been Ivan Wagner (The Patron), Robert Kessler, Hans Grüter and Rolf Ringdal. It was a great thrill when Robert invited me to become an associate member of the SAS in 1996.

Skiing is a sociable activity, and the Eighties were a time for making the most of every day and enjoying the company of Kandahar friends including George Woodruff, Andrew Nelson, Kim Palmer and the Lunn brothers. George has never raced much but he skis sublimely and to me he is the British equivalent of the great all-round skier with whom I shared many adventures in the high Alps, Ernst von Allmen of Stechelberg.

Ernst was the most elegant of skiers, good company and never at a loss for a story to tell about the filming of 'On Her Majesty's Secret Service' in 1968. He skied countless hours for the camera on the higher slopes of Mürren and the Petersgrat glacier, but his payday came when he was hired to play the part of a British agent's corpse, swinging on a rope upside down outside the Piz Gloria restaurant.

Robert Kessler

Paula Boyagis, pretty in powder. Photo: Nick Morgan

Bernie Lunn (left) presenting his older brother Stevie with the Arnold Lunn medal in 2016

Andrew Nelson was an extremely flexible skier, brilliant through the moguls in his younger days, an excellent jumper and an accomplished Inferno racer. He and Royston Varley were witnesses to a narrow escape of mine when we were training for the Inferno together more than twenty years ago. In those days the race started higher up the mountain and we used to take it straight from above the corner of the Schilthorn. I was leading, went over the small jump before the first traverse and, feeling quite comfortable in the air, looked down and to my horror saw that only my right ski was attached to its boot. With the big rock face fast approaching I knew what I had to do. It was essential that I slid feet first, so I slipped onto my left side, keeping my right ski in the air, and used my left boot as a brake. Luckily it went to plan, and I stopped a few metres from the rock. "That was interesting," said Andrew. I knew how fortunate I had been.

Kim is the one of the world's most relaxed people, great fun on and off the mountain; he particularly enjoyed my stag party in 1994. For years - perhaps decades - the Inferno was suggested to him and he always found a reason why Mürren in the middle of January could not possibly fit into his diary. But when his sister Melanie signed up for the 2018 race, it became avoidable no longer, and they both raced well.

Skiing with the Lunn brothers, Stevie and Bernie, was always fun: they had such contrasting styles. Stevie was strong, fast and fearless with his weight slightly further back than many skiers would feel comfortable with. Bernie was almost as quick, and rather more stylish; we spent many happy hours skiing powder together. Stylish skiing brings Paula Boyagis to mind: an outstanding slalom racer and a pleasure to watch in the powder.

I made many exciting off-piste trips with Walter Amstutz in the high Alps. Being two years younger than the century, he was a veteran by this time, but his agility, fitness and skill were undimmed and a joy to watch. And he was a fund of good stories.

One trip with Walter and Franz Sonderegger saw us helicoptered to the Ebnefluh and Petersgrat in March 1983 on a day blessed with sunshine and every conceivable snow condition, mostly good. Towards the end of the run down from Petersgrat, our local guide paused at the top of the so-called Black Forest, and said in Swiss German: "Be careful here - if you fall you will slide a very long way." Seconds later he crossed his tips and showed us exactly what not to do.

After checking that the guide was fine, Walter found the situation hilarious and said, "perfect demonstration, no charge." On arriving at the Hotel Stechelberg, we tucked into Bündnerfleisch (air-dried mountain beef), Hobelkäse (planed mountain cheese) and excellent wine. Over dinner with Walter and Eveline in their chalet that evening, I thanked Walter for the trip of a lifetime. "The first trip of a lifetime!" he said, and of course he was right. Later that week we had another great day off-piste together, including my first experience of skiing down the Saustal. The entrance to this valley along the north western ridge of the Schilthorn requires concentration and a good head for heights. I have skied it many times since, and always think of that day with Walter.

Through him I was privileged to meet many skiers from the pre-War period, often called the Golden Age of Skiing. Few had longer memories than Godi Michel who had been Tourist Director in Mürren more than 50 years before I met him. He set up one of Switzerland's first ski schools in Mürren in 1930, with an advanced badge system to show a skier's level.

I enjoyed memorable off-piste days and heliski trips with the engaging and energetic Arnold (Noldi) Kaech, particularly in March 1989. Noldi had been the most senior officer in the Swiss army, an accomplished racer for SAS either side of the Second World War and an excellent cross-country skier. He was a great supporter of the Kandahar and a highly respected Chairman of Schilthornbahn AG.

Godi Michel, ski racer and far sighted Mürren Kurdirektor

Ian Munro

Godi Michel

Kurt Huggler jumps the Hundschopf in the 1968 Lauberhorn at Wengen. Kurt was leading the race but fell near the finish

Bernhard Russi, World Cup Downhill Champion 1971 and 1972

Noldi Kaech above the Saustal, 1989

Roland Collombin, World Cup Downhill Chamion 1973 and 1974

*My slalom hero Ingemar
Stenmark's second run World
Cup charges were legendary*

*Franz Klammer on course for his most famous win, in the
Olympic Downhill at Igls, 1976*

Noldi hosted parties for his Mürren friends and was always wonderful company. It was through him that I got to know Ian Munro, a great character who had raced with Peter Lunn and Jimmy Riddell in the lead-up to the Garmisch Winter Olympics of 1936.

In March 1989 I met up with Ian, Noldi and a close friend of Ian's who later became a good friend of mine, Humphrey Ronn, for breakfast at the Schilthorn. It was obvious that although he was skiing well, Ian's health was failing. Humphrey and I had decided that it would be lovely for the two old friends, Noldi and Ian, to enjoy a few runs together. I am pleased they did, as they never skied together again.

Ian grabbed my arm and thanked me, with a warning that Humphrey might need assistance to get down the Schilthorn. He was right, but Humphrey was stoic and determined, and we made it down …. eventually. As Anthony Ayles reminded me recently, Ian used to say 'schiing', not 'skiing' - a charming throwback to the early Golden Age of Skiing. Within two years Ian had died: a true gentleman, always interesting and interested in others irrespective of age.

My early ski heroes were the likes of Bernhard Russi, Roland Collombin and Franz Klammer in skiing's blue riband event, the Downhill, and Ingemar Stenmark in Slalom and GS. I was introduced to Franz Klammer as a keen young skier in early January 1975, just before his victory in Wengen's classic Downhill, the Lauberhorn. My parents and I, along with the entire Austrian team, were staying in the Hotel Alpenrose in Wengen for Lauberhorn race week. The longest downhill on the World Cup circuit has every racing challenge imaginable, as well as the breath-taking Oberland scenery - not that the racers have time to appreciate it.

Every keen skier of my age remembers Franz Klammer's amazingly brave run at his home Olympics in Innsbruck in 1976. Wearing bib number 15, Klammer risked everything to pip Bernhard Russi to the Gold Medal.

Klammer's run was a great boost for the popularity of skiing around the world and particularly in Great Britain, where the BBC's Grandstand coverage with David Vine and Ron Pickering was watched by millions. The BBC's coverage of those Winter Olympics led to the creation of Ski Sunday in 1978: television moments that inspired me to take up downhill racing in the early 1980s.

Jimmy Riddel - a man of all the talents, and great charm

Inferno!

For the last three and a half decades - more than half my life - the Inferno has been a passion of mine and the highlight of my skiing year. Should any of my readers need reminding, this annual event is a long-distance downhill race from the Schilthorn to Lauterbrunnen, founded - and memorably named - by a group of Kandahar members in January 1928.

There were 17 racers that day, including 4 women, and Harold Mitchell won in a time of 1 hour and 12 minutes. These days the Inferno is a public race for around 1800 competitors. and more than 3000 amateur skiers apply to take part every year. Over a nine-mile course, with sections of uphill skiing, the challenge is to be fit and to race as close to the limit of one's ability as possible.

One who shares my interest is Andrew Morgan, a Kandahar stalwart who with the Club's help published The Inferno Story in 2009. This history of the race enjoys pride of place on the skiing shelves in my library. Andrew was painstakingly forensic in his research and tells the story brilliantly. I commend it to anyone interested in the race. I will not repeat his words, but must pay a personal tribute to Jimmy Riddell, a charming man of many and various talents who won the 1929 Inferno in remarkable circumstances.

I first met Jimmy when I was in my early twenties. Like Ian Munro, an exact contemporary of his, Jimmy was always interesting and interested. A brilliant all-round sportsman and athlete in his youth, he later wrote a hatful of books on skiing and ski resorts, was a fine artist, a great raconteur and always good company.

Jimmy came to Mürren in 1993 for the occasion of the 50th Inferno, and was interviewed by a British journalist. I listened in and made a recording of his memories of the 1929 race. Here is Jimmy's account:

"I first came to Mürren when I was 9 years old in 1919. My father had fought through the desert war in the Great War and he was so fed up with sand that he wanted to see the exact opposite, so they bought me to Mürren so that I could learn to ski. The first thing that astonished me was the scenery of the Bernese Oberland. I stayed in this very hotel where I am being interviewed now, the Eiger Hotel, and it is where I had my tenth birthday. This village of Mürren has not changed very much. It has maintained its wonderful Swiss character with its chalets up on its sunny shelf above the Lauterbrunnen valley. The atmosphere here is much as it was in the old days. You walked about - no cars - and you made friends with all the villagers. There was a tremendous rapport between the Swiss and the British. The Swiss were very patient with us, because we used to ski over all their fences and their back gardens and they didn't seem to mind which was very good.

By 1929 I had become reasonably good at skiing. For some reason I could not make the first Inferno race in 1928 and when I came out in 1929 I entered the race and it just so happened I won it. But as far as I was concerned it was the most glorious adventure. It was the first time that I had climbed on ski up to the 10,000 foot mark and there the Bernese Oberland was even more spectacular. I thoroughly enjoyed this race, it was then the toughest race there was. There were no control gates, there wasn't the nice equipment that you have today, the skis were primitive, there was no piste, there were no flags, there were no safety nets if you made a monkey of it. You started off in a mass start, we used to call it the geschmozzle start. It was the most lovely adventure - very exhausting, but still ….

The difference today from the conditions that we had is, for every 1000 feet we skied downhill, we had to climb up on foot and to get to the start of this race on the top of the Schilthorn (involved climbing) through deep, untracked snow. It was really quite an effort.

We started at six in the morning and it took us four or five hours to get up there. We then had to take off such clothing that we wanted to get rid of and give it to a chap with a rucksack. We took our skins off and waxed our skis and then we were off. The way these races in those days were timed was by stopwatch, there was no electronic timing or telephone. In the morning of the race the starter and the finisher synchronised their stop watches and then the starter went to the top of the mountain and the finishing crew went down to the very bottom, right down in the valley.

This really was a monster race, dropping all but 7500 feet. The race went through every kind of condition: high altitude snow, then through tracked snows and then was a langlauf section to Grütschalp and then was a very difficult section down from Grütschalp to Lauterbrunnen. It was unmarked, there were many tight corners, the trees were very close together with steep slopes between them, never more than 3 metres between them, there were wood chutes and very steep icy paths - every conceivable kind of difficulty. That took you right down to Lauterbrunnen. It was the longest and toughest race that there was. But I had trained on it and I knew it backwards.

When I got to the finishing post, there was absolutely nobody in sight, it was the little square in Lauterbrunnen, there was nobody there at all, no time keepers, no finish judges. I was there, covered in snow from head to foot without any notion of where anybody was. After a bit of looking around I decided that they must be in the pub. So I went rushing across to the Sternen and I bashed the door open, I went through the dining room where people were having their lunch, looking very stately.

Major Riddell, wartime skilehrer at The Cedars of Lebanon

This figure of a snowman, covered in snow, on skis with sticks, suddenly went clattering by all the tables of the restaurant. I rushed out to the back, past the kitchen and in the back room I found them all having their glass of Dunkles Bier and they leapt to their feet in astonishment. And they said "you have no right to be here, what are you doing? You can't be here!" "Well," I said, "I am here." They took my time then, in the back room, and rushed out into the square to take the times of the other people. They were sitting there because they weren't expecting me for half an hour, so I did actually beat the first time of the race by 30 minutes. Imagine it!'

In 1931 Jimmy came 4th in the slalom at the inaugural Alpine Skiing World Championships in Mürren, and he was the top racer at the Anglo-Swiss races that winter. He was British Ski Champion in 1934/35 and vice-captain of the British Winter Olympic team in 1936. From 1941 - 44 Major Riddell, as he then was, ran the Middle East Ski and Mountaineering School at the Cedars of Lebanon, where as Chief Instructor he trained more than 20,000 Allied soldiers to ski and survive at high altitude. For this work he was awarded an MBE. Jimmy's important contribution to British skiing and the respect he enjoyed are reflected in the fact that at various times he served as President of the Alpine Ski Club, the Kandahar Ski Club and the Ski Club of Great Britain.

After the death of his first wife Jimmy married Ali, a former Mürren chalet girl who was the 1994 Times Cook of the Year. A meal at Foresters, the Riddell home in the New Forest, has always been a treat. The story of his Inferno win in 1929 inspired me to come up with the idea of the James Riddell Medal a few years after his death at the age of 90 in 2000. Ali agreed that a medal in memory of Jimmy for the top K lady and man on a full-length Inferno race would be a fitting tribute to a great man. Ali designed and generously bought the medals which were first presented in 2006.

Enjoying perfect weather for the 2003 Inferno. Photo: Beatrice Gertsch

Jimmy Riddell in Lebanese powder

Geschmozzle start

I took part in my first Inferno in March 1986, shortly before my father's death. It was a selfish relief for me, as I could take my mind off my poor father for a week; his untimely death took me a long time to recover from. That first Inferno in January 1986 was a truly British affair, wet and foggy. The race piste was bumpy, but despite this difficult first experience my commitment to this great race soon became a fixture and a fixation. Since then I have managed, at the time of writing (in 2018), to enter and complete the race on 32 consecutive occasions, the only gap being 1990, when the race was postponed from January until April, then cancelled. I still have plenty of racing to do, before catching up with Franz Sonderegger who raced the Inferno 54 times and died a few days before his 55th.

The Inferno is always slightly different and over time the course has changed. In my early days we started 100 metres below the summit of the Schilthorn; now (weather and snow permitting) it starts some 200 metres lower than that. In the 1980s the top section of the course was a steep mogul field; today's Inferno piste is beautifully prepared and marked. Almost all my races have been great fun, packed with physical challenge and exhilaration.

I have raced on 12 different courses, starting at Schilthorn, Birg, Allmendhubel and the Hog's Back, with finishes at Kanonenrohr, Allmendhubel, Mürren, Winteregg, Pletschenalp (mid-way between Winteregg and Grütschalp), Alpweg (a meadow 280m above the Lauterbrunnen finish area) and Lauterbrunnen itself. The highest start was 26 metres below the 2970m summit of the Schilthorn on a warm winter's day in 1987. The finish that day was in Lauterbrunnen (800m), giving a height differential of 2144 metres - plus a few for the two uphill sections - for a course of more than 15km. The 2018 Inferno - a 2.35km course from Allmendhubel to Mürren with a vertical drop of only 280m - was a different experience, and a great disappointment in a year of abundant snowfall; not to be repeated, I earnestly hope.

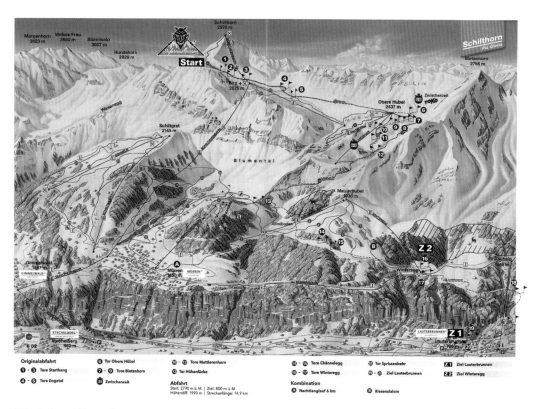

The Inferno Race Course

Nearly at the finish of the shortest-ever Inferno, 2018

After a couple of races it dawned on me that despite being quite fast I needed to improve my technique if I was to challenge the top Kandahar places in the Inferno. For helping me with this, I will always be grateful to Heini Messner, a retired Austrian racer who won bronze in the Giant Slalom at the 1968 Winter Olympics and bronze in the Downhill four years later, behind the two Swiss greats, Russi and Collombin. On an Austrian glacier in October 1987 Heini completely overhauled my technique and after race training each day I flew down the mountain behind him. I learnt a huge amount and won the race training camp gold medal. I have never forgotten, and won't forget, those autumn training days more than thirty years ago.

In my fifties it is inconceivable that I will again make a top three finish out of all 150+ Kandahar racers in the Inferno, but I am proud of my podium places and my win in 1997, which put my name alongside Konrad Bartelski's on the John Palmer Memorial Trophy.

Looking back on the last three decades, my Inferno memories are overwhelmingly positive. I have made scores of good friends during Inferno week and by and large encountered great sportsmanship. The people of Mürren and its neighbouring villages around the valley have skilfully and thoughtfully run the Inferno since 1936.

The father of the race we know and enjoy today is Kurt Huggler, who had the vision to broaden the appeal of the Downhill and added Langlauf and Giant Slalom races for an Inferno Combination over four days. In his drive to push for progress with the Inferno, Kurt could always count on the support of Fritz Stäger of Lauterbrunnen, a lovely man with a progressive outlook and a great sense of humour who had won the Inferno either side of World War Two. Kurt remembers the time his close friend told a press conference: "normally two Stägers have together three heads, but Huggler has alone two heads."

Kurt Huggler made the Inferno what it is today

Peter Bühler

When Kurt was elevated to Honorary President in 1994, Peter Bühler took on the mantle of working President of the Inferno's organising committee. He nurtured and improved Kurt's creation, and both have had invaluable support in the office from the hard-working, efficient and unfailingly helpful Sandra Herren, who now works with the no less conscientious Manuela Kohler. We racers are indebted to them for making the Inferno such a great festival of amateur sport. The only sadness is that the years come around far too quickly.

In the late 1980s the Kandahar Captain was Stephen Lunn, with me in support, officially as Vice-Captain from 1991. At that time the Kandahar Race Programme was put together by Ted Varley, who always encouraged me.

I enjoyed helping Ted organise the skiing events that we now know as Kandahar Inferno Race Week - the build-up to the Inferno and a highlight of the Club's year. Ted's instruction and guidance during these weeks, which in those days used to follow the Inferno, held me in good stead for the future.

Ted's programme for 1987 reintroduced a K Slalom, GS and a Downhill 'of old'. This off-piste race started at Dogger Rock some 100 metres above the top of the Winteregg chairlift, took a line to the left of the red piste, down Peter Lunn Gully to a flat area where we skated uphill to the red run and then dived off left into the trees before a final schuss over the Witching Waves to the finish by Half-Way House (Winteregg).

Setting the course on the day before this old-fashioned race, we had trudged through deep snow to set the start at Dogger Rock, followed by another five off-piste gates to the finish at Winteregg. The weather forecast was good for the next 48 hours, but by the following morning four and a half feet of snow had fallen.

Arriving at the top with twenty racers, we could find little trace of our course, but after much floundering in neck-deep snow the race finally took place and everyone enjoyed

Prince and Princess Chichibu at Grindelwald in 1937

With my first Kandahar cup, the
Prince Chichibu Trophy, 1987

Pippa Middleton in the Inferno Langlauf, 2016.
Photo: Beatrice Gertsch

Adam Ruck enjoys the powder

the yesteryear experience. I certainly did: having climbed into a lead on the hill, I was thrilled to hang on to it until the finish and win by 21 seconds. A few days later I got my hands on the beautiful Prince Chichibu Bowl, my first Kandahar trophy.

This cup had been given by His Imperial Highness Prince Chichibu of Japan, the younger brother of Emperor Hirohito. Prince Chichibu was Oxford-educated, pro-British and vehemently opposed to Japan's stance in the war. He argued against his older brother's stance of an alliance with Hitler's Germany against the United States and Great Britain. History might have been quite different, had he been the older brother.

Chichibu was a regular visitor to Mürren and a good friend of Arnold Lunn and Walter Amstutz. He was known as the Sporting Prince due to his love of mountaineering, skiing and rugby, and Japan's premier rugby stadium is named after him. In 1926 he was offered honorary membership of the Kandahar but declined, preferring to be an ordinary member on merit - a sporting gesture, as Arnold Lunn wrote in the Kandahar Review, "typical of one of the best sportsmen who has ever visited Mürren. The Prince is a very good ski-runner and an ardent mountaineer." His health started to fail when he contracted pulmonary tuberculosis in his late 30s. He recovered to a certain extent but was only 50 when he died in 1953.

When Stephen Lunn retired as Captain in 1993, I was invited to take over, a position I held for 7 years. My aim was simple: to increase participation in amateur ski racing, particularly within the Kandahar Ski Club. I had the help of many good friends and in particular (and in chronological order) Frank Casimir, Simon (Sam) Hulse and Nick Morgan. Between us we devised a programme that slowly grew, filling the week before the Inferno Downhill with ski races interspersed with sledging, curling and drinks parties. The format proved popular and from a dozen or so racers in the mid - 1980s, the number of Kandahar Inferno participants had grown to over 100 by my last year as Captain.

Kandahar membership was also growing during these years, not only because of the Inferno race week programme, but also because activity levels in the Club grew. Few ski racing clubs in the world have a heritage comparable to Kandahar's, but clubs cannot live on past glories. They need to be forward thinking, relevant and creative.

UK media interest in Inferno week began in the mid - '80s and has gathered pace since then. Paula Boyagis arranged for Clive James to come for the Inferno in 1985, for a TV programme that never aired, because of the weather. Peter Hardy and John Hopkins took part in my first Inferno year, 1986, and wrote contrasting articles for the Express and The Sunday Times, reproduced in the Kandahar Review. Roger Alton came for The Spectator, Neil English for The Mail. Alistair Scott, Minty Clinch and Adam Ruck became regular attendees from the mid - '90s and Adam has recently taken over from Melanie Byrom as Editor of the Kandahar Review. Many of these journalists became Kandahar members and friends and most of them have written positive words about Mürren, the Kandahar and Inferno race week.

Thanks to these promotional efforts from inside and outside the Kandahar, UK participation in the Inferno has risen from about 2% in the late '80s to nearly 15%, including 180+ Kandahar members in 2018.

In 2016 media interest reached a new frenzied level due to the presence - as Inferno competitor and Hello! columnist - of Pippa Middleton, as she then was. Pippa had friends who were regular visitors to Mürren for Inferno week and being the sporty girl that she is, the Inferno was on her bucket list.

On Wednesday evening she smiled most of the way round the Inferno Langlauf circuit and her smile widened when people in the crowd shouted "come on Pippa!" I can't remember a racer before or since radiating such warmth while participating in such an arduous sport.

The next day it fell to me to guide Pippa down the Downhill run a few times, and she was a delight to help: a great listener who left no stone unturned in her determination to race as well as possible. There was a lot for her to take in, as there is for any Inferno newcomer, and in the afternoon Pippa asked if we could take another look at the 'gun barrel' above the Blattwang. I agreed, hit a bump as I flew around the corner, lost a ski, landed hard on my shoulder and slid 50 metres down the Blattwang. Pippa quickly came to my aid and passed me the missing ski. As many others have found before, a compaction injury of the shoulder takes a year to recover from, irrespective of age.

That evening Pippa came along to a drinks party at our chalet and, as I had acquired a couple of catsuits for her to try, I offered her our bedroom as a changing room. After a few minutes she called out my name so I entered the room and there she was, sporting the first catsuit. It looked good but not exactly close-fitting. "Pippa, do you want it a little …. loose?" I asked. "I do not want it baggy!" she fired back, so I offered up a ridiculously small purple catsuit for her to try. Before long she summoned me back in for another viewing. "Oh yes!" I said. Perfect.

She was great fun all week, raced well in the Inferno and danced with a few lucky Kandahar members in the early hours of Sunday morning. They might even have included a balding man with a sore shoulder …. or was I dreaming? I hope Pippa makes it back to Mürren again one day.

As Captain I put a lot of effort into welcoming new skiers and Kandahar friends to the thrills of Inferno week. Simon Hulse helped me develop a spring newsletter with the results from the previous season combined with the following season's programme, along with newspaper cuttings that related to the Inferno. Many racers came back year after year.

Nobody skis deep powder better than Sam Hulse   Ted Varley

Viscount Montgomery of Alamein making a presentation to Ted Varley

Simon invited me to join him on my first Canadian heli-skiing trip in the late winter of 1991/92. Despite being a March/April week it was terrific fun and I went twice more in the years leading up to 'Dwina's and my wedding in December 1994.

I had first met Simon Hulse in the mid - 1980s and much enjoyed his company on the slopes of Mürren. Sam, as his friends know him, is an interesting character - very bright, loyal and giving to his friends, but quite reserved on first meeting.

When Ted Varley passed the organisation of the newly formed Inferno Kandahar race week to Stevie and me in 1989, Sam's skills, very different from mine, were a great asset. We made a good team. Sam had his own bulwark in Lucy, the kindest and most considerate wife. Always smiling and positive even when life was tough, Lucy was a great mother to their three children, and her death in 2016 came without warning, a terrible blow from the blind side.

Ted Varley's death in 1996 was also unexpected and a great shock to his family and many friends in Mürren. I sent a long and emotional letter to Ted's lovely wife Aliki that summer, mentioning all my early memories of him. I'll never forget Ted's support during my first Inferno week.

The Giant Slalom and Inferno downhill were not really the problem, it was the Langlauf or in my case 'shortlauf.' I practised this new pursuit along the railway line to Winteregg, returned gingerly along the bottom road and fell over outside the Varley shop. With Ted now peering out of the window, I tried to get up too quickly and got into an even greater tangle. Once he stopped laughing, Ted set about organising Langlauf instruction for me, and I could not have wished for better instructors: Noldi Kaech and Alfred Guggisberg.

Apart from being a fine skier, Ted was no slouch with a tennis racket in hand. On one winter's evening I was invited along to see the new 'tennis-ball' machine in action. It soon developed a mind of its own and sprayed one hundred balls all around the Sports Centre Hall - into the floor, the roof, the windows .... Ted and I beat a hasty retreat.

A couple of years after Ted died, I approached his widow Aliki and their children Chloë and Royston and suggested that a trophy in Ted's memory would celebrate his contribution to Mürren and the Kandahar.

We already had enough cups for the main Kandahar competitions; what was missing was a cup - or a bowl, as it turned out - for both ladies and gentlemen and for all ages for something that was close to Ted's heart and that was for an outstanding performance in the Inferno. It was awarded for the first time in 1999, the Club's 75th anniversary year, and the recipients were Peter Lunn and his grandson Will Lunn.

Away from Kandahar race week, I had overseen the engraving of the wonderful collection of old Kandahar cups, many of which had been raced for until the 1960s, then mothballed. Other cups had not been engraved since the early 1930s.

Gilfrid Day, past Chairman and President of the Kandahar, created a 'Black Book' filled with detail about all our historic trophies. He and I consulted regularly to ensure that cups were correctly engraved and we discussed how they might be brought back into service as race week activities grew. In due course Gilfrid passed this role on to another retired Chairman and President, Andrew Morgan.

Before long most of the Club's historic cups were back in use, but it became evident that too many of them were being concentrated in too few hands. How to spread them around? Simon Hulse had the idea of rewarding improvement from one Inferno to the next, for teams of four and individual racers. It was a useful addition, giving many rank-and-file racers the chance to win Kandahar silverware for the first time.

The Hulse-Palmer Cup has filled an important gap.

I have always enjoyed helping first timers with their Inferno; I must have advised more than 1000 newcomers over the years. My tips have centred on giving the right advice to racers so that they achieve the best result for their ability. I maintain that the Inferno is about fitness, concentration and ensuring that you ski the slow parts fast and not about trying to ski the fast parts beyond one's ability level. The slow parts are the paths and the climbs, where ski preparation, ski base and the length of poles are key. It never fails to amaze me how many average racers have the desire to put on a pair of 225cm downhill racing skis. Tactfully I try to explain the reasons why they would probably be 5 minutes faster on a pair of well-prepared GS skis.

One funny moment occurred on a snowy morning, the day before the Inferno. The light was flat and at that time the race started just above where it does today. The first 60 metres was a slow left-hand bend just to the Birg side of the main Schilthorn piste. We had glided around the corner and I had started to recap on the first big test of the race, having discussed ski pole length, mindset etc …. I asked one of the assembled throng to be back marker, as there were 12 of us. But when I counted, there were 11 - we had been there no more than a couple of minutes and had somehow lost a racer in the first 60 metres. At which point a snowman came into the view, declaring loudly "thank …. that bit is out of the way." Trevor Evans has always been tremendous fun to be with, whether in the mountains or anywhere else: kind, generous and, when it came to the Inferno, brave. A decade earlier I was witness on two occasions when safety netting disappeared from the side of the mountain attached to his binding.

One snowy lunchtime I took refuge in the Hotel Bellevue with a group of friends including Ben Whitmore, whose father Simon founded the successful Butcombe Brewery. One member of the group - I'll call him X - unaware of the connection, said how much he enjoyed our brewery's beers and country pubs, before suddenly adding: "who on earth named a Somerset brewery Butcombe? What a stupid name

Trevor Evans, hanging on. Photo: Edwina Palmer   *Ed Killwick*

With Jonathan Botting at the top of the Schilthorn, June 20th 2016

for a brewery!"

It was an awkward moment. The table had gone quiet, with Ben sitting two chairs away. I quickly said, "well, it's the village where the brewery is based, and I guess you have not met Ben Whitmore, the son of the founder of Butcombe Brewery." X banged his head on the table and groaned. To everyone's great relief, Ben laughed it off. As it happens, I have always considered Butcombe rather a good name for a brewery.

One morning I bumped into a group of young trainees on the Schilthorn. I had my downhill skis with me - the weather was fabulous, the piste was in great condition, and I had decided to have an Inferno warm-up run. The children's trainer asked me to show them my Inferno line, which I did, then stopped and waited at the end of the first traverse for the young group to arrive. The children were excited but when I took off my helmet to have a longer chat they went quiet. I could see that most of them were looking at me in bewilderment, and I realised why when one boy blurted out that I was older than his grandfather. After a moment I said, "if you are lucky with your health and you feel fit, the trick is not to look in the mirror."

Jonathan Botting, a great doctor and RCGP Clinical Champion in minor surgery, is one of the world's great enthusiasts and has brightened up the last twenty Inferno weeks. We have enjoyed many glorious Swiss powder days together, and the same goes for Ed Killwick, another Inferno regular and a great friend down the years. Ed is a good team leader who loves the fun of the off-piste but is always alert to the potential dangers. Jonathan, Ed and I had a memorable off-piste holiday in Zermatt in late April 2016, blessed with perfect snow and weather.

Every alpine holiday is improved if it includes Filippo Guerrini-Maraldi or Anthony Ayles, or preferably both. Apart from being good friends of mine, they are good friends of each other; great fun on the mountain and masters of après ski. Filippo is a good racer who loves a party; he has great style on the racing piste and off the mountain. As a junior, Anthony was one of Britain's finest young skiers. He was British Universities ski champion on three occasions and captained the BUSC team to victory in the 50th Anglo Swiss. My cousin Walter Amstutz, who was the successful Captain in the 1st Anglo Swiss all those years before, was there to congratulate him. In 2018 Anthony proved that he still has the speed, style and skill of a much younger man when he won the Kandahar slalom during Inferno week. No one approaching 50 had won it before, let alone over 60.

Nick Morgan is a formidably well-organised, thoughtful and intelligent man. As our friendship developed it became apparent to me that he was a future Chairman of the Kandahar, with all the right skills. I was delighted when that came to pass after my five-year term came to an end in 2011. Away from Kandahar life, Nick, his glamorous wife Carolyn and their children spent many happy family holidays with us and Sophie and Mark in a variety of child-friendly Alpine villages. We all hoped our children would develop a passion for ski sport, and they all did.

After the tour. Jonathan Botting and Ed Killwick, Zermatt, April 10th 2016

Nifty at sixty; Anthony Ayles. Photo: Toby Carless

Party animal; Filippo Guerrini-Maraldi in his element at the AICC. Photo: Nick Morgan

Carolyn Morgan and 'Dwina Palmer

Nigel, Jane and Richard Fawkes, Mürren 2018

Christoph Egger

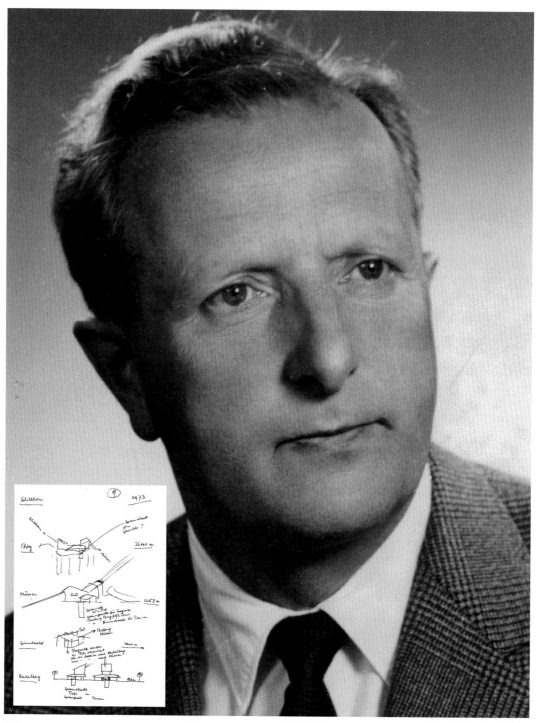

Above: Ernst Feuz, ski champion and father of the Schilthornbahn
Inset: Ernst Feuz's sketch of the Schilthorn cable-car project. The top section opened on 12th June 1967

After more than a decade running the Inferno Kandahar race week, with great support from Nick and Sam Hulse, it was time to hand over the baton to a younger racer and I was delighted when Anna Lees-Jones (now Griffin) accepted the role in 2000. When Nick's father Andrew called me a few months later to say the Kandahar Board had decided to award me the Arnold Lunn medal for services to skiing, for once I was lost for words. Receiving the medal from Peter Lunn was a proud moment.

Anna further broadened the week by introducing many of her numerous skiing friends. She was a great racer and is still the only Kandahar lady to have been the Club's Inferno champion. After five years at the helm, and a hiatus when I stood in as Inferno Week Captain in 2006, she made way for Richard Fawkes in 2007. Richard is another excellent racer: Combined Services Downhill Champion in 2005 and, like Anna, winner of many Kandahar trophies. He is also a charming leader who has been Captain for a record number of years. Unfortunately, work pressures in the RAF have occasionally kept him away from our main race week.

Mürren must be one of the prettiest villages in the world, perched on a sunny shelf above the Lauterbrunnen valley with stunning views of the north wall of the Alps. As Jimmy Riddell said in the interview I quoted earlier, Mürren had not really changed much since his first visit in 1919. This is of course partly the key to Mürren's success: careful investment without undue modernisation.

Much of the credit for Mürren's success over the last fifty years is due to Ernst Feuz, a native of Mürren who knew what was best for his home village. He was the father and initiator of the Schilthorn cableway, and through his vision, determination and business connections carried this massive project through to completion. Ernst was a close friend of Walter Amstutz and I was privileged to meet him on a few occasions.

It has been fantastic to see the recent investments made by Schilthornbahn AG: new lifts, improved lifts, new ski and toboggan runs, a snow park .... the list goes on. For all

Werner Zimmerli at the 2016 AICC

A retirement gift for Ueli Frei, Mürren's chief of pistes, March 2011. Photo: Mark Palmer

this we are immensely grateful to the driving force behind the Schilthornbahn of today, Christoph Egger, a highly committed and focused leader with a steely determination to drive the business in the right direction. Christoph is now President of the Inferno Organising Committee.

A key member of his team at the Schilthornbahn is Alan Ramsay, a genial friend to many who have visited Mürren through the last three decades - and not just to the British. Alan started life in Mürren as a barman and a fearless skier. He soon became adept at both, spent time in hotel management and now has the perfect job as the Schilthornbahn's Head of Sales, with an international remit that extends from the UK to China. Luckily he enjoys travelling.

Mürren is a second home to my family and we have always been made to feel welcome there, as have so many visitors from around the world. I and other Kandahar members have always tried to work closely with the villagers when organising our Club races. When I was Kandahar Captain and later when we hosted the first two Amateur Inter-Club Championships (AICC) in Mürren, Peter Bühler and his team of race organisers could not have been more supportive and sympathetic to this new Championship's needs. Without their support the AICC would not have got off the ground.

Over the last three decades, many lasting friendships have been forged in Mürren. Adrian Stähli, Werner Zimmerli (a great racer and owner of the three excellent Stäger Sports shops), Kurt Huggler, Peter Bühler, Ueli Frei, Alan Ramsay, Andy Meyer, Toni Brunner, Othmar Suter of the excellent Hotel Bellevue, Christoph Egger .... not forgetting their better halves. Without their friendship and support, life in this wonderful Alpine haven would have been infinitely less enjoyable.

With the Duke of Kent and Nick Morgan. Photo: Nick Marden

At the helm

To many Kandahar members, who turn out now and again for a blast of ski racing fun and gratefully pack their children off for junior training, the Club may seem an uncomplicated association of like-minded enthusiasts, requiring little more than someone to organise the races and someone else to collect subscriptions.

In fact, the smooth running of the Club requires a huge amount of work behind the scenes - legal issues, insurance, finance, child protection, data protection, membership administration, sport politics - and that requires a team of all the talents, led by a Chairman with an overview and an eye to the future. The Kandahar board meets regularly through the year, and the agenda for its meetings is always full. I never fail to be impressed by the depth and breadth of expertise our directors bring to the table, and the amount of work they put in - all pro bono.

After seven years as Captain my turn came to do a five-year stint as Chairman - a great honour, and all the more enjoyable for being part of an excellent team. Annette Hughes (Hon Secretary), Andrew Carless (Hon Treasurer) and Nick Morgan (Vice Chairman) were at the heart of it and my predecessor Bobby Cohen was always there with wise advice when required. Together, we achieved a lot.

The Kandahar is privileged to have had three Royal Patrons. The Duke of Kent's patronage goes back to 1968 - more than half the life of The Club. His parents were Patrons before him.

Annette Hughes, Hon Sec of the Kandahar for twenty years

Kandahar members including the Earl of Wessex at the Club's 90th Birthday party, Jan 2014

I made sure that HRH was invited to my first AGM as Chairman. He accepted and duly presided over the 2007 AGM. One notable achievement of that year was the implementation of what I call the 'Nick Morgan Report' into how the future relationship between the Club and Kandahar Racing should be. This excellent report paved the way for the success that K Racing enjoys today under Matt Shepherd's management. I was also able to announce that after much planning the inaugural Amateur Inter-Club Championship (AICC) would take place in Mürren in March 2008.

I had met Prince Edward a few times before the Kandahar Board decided to offer him and the Countess of Wessex honorary membership. They are both keen skiers and the Earl in particular enjoys skiing the piste at high speed, as I found out when he stayed with us in 2014 for the Kandahar's 90th birthday celebrations. The formal presentation took place in Méribel on 27th March 2007 during the British Championships. Beat Hodler, the Club's President at the time, bestowed the Honorary Memberships on Their Royal Highnesses at a splendid dinner in the Hotel Allodis, with the proviso that they should continually strive to improve their skiing. From what I have seen and heard, they have done just that.

In 2008 Annette Hughes took charge of reforming first February and then Christmas/New Year junior training in Mürren. The key to the success of this was Mark Berry's wonderfully charismatic and inspiring leadership on the mountain. A generation of Kandahar children, including our two, adored skiing at Mürren with Mark, the Kandahar's own Pied Piper, on and off the piste. They learnt a huge amount from him and, whatever the weather, he always made it fun.

Mark Berry

Kandahar board members past and present, 2007

It was during my years as Club Captain that the thought - which soon became a plan - hatched in my mind, that the Kandahar should rekindle relationships with other like-minded ski clubs whose members were keen on amateur racing. These close relationships had started with the birth of the Arlberg Kandahar (AK) race meetings in 1928 but had lapsed with the spread of professionalism.

The AK races, which Arnold Lunn and Hannes Schneider had originally conceived as a twinning between St Anton and Mürren, grew to embrace all the Alpine nations with the addition to the rota of Chamonix, Sestriere and Garmisch. Before the World Cup was born in 1967, these annual races were Alpine skiing's blue riband events. They fuelled the technical development of ski racing, and firm friendships were forged between the clubs in the host resorts.

Soon after my five-year term as Kandahar Chairman began, I requested and received Board approval to launch the Amateur Inter-Club Championship – the AICC. Over the 18 months before the inaugural event in March 2008 I contacted all the AK clubs as well as a variety of newer ski racing clubs. Since then we have successfully staged 11 championships, and in that time more than 15 clubs have participated, the core being SC Arlberg (Austria), Alpbach Visitors SC (GB & Austria), SC 18 and Sci Accademico Italiano (Italy), SAS & Eagle SC (Switzerland), Kandahar, DHO & Marden's (GB & Switzerland) and Ladies SC (GB). Key to the success of the AICC has been its international flavour and the commitment of its International Organising Committee whose members I can't thank enough.

Annette Hughes is the crux of it: Secretary, Webmaster and lead contact. The AICC's Vice President, James Palmer-Tomkinson, handles sponsorship and was an excellent Championship host in Klosters (Marden's 2014). I am equally grateful to the AICC's other hosts: Clemente Reale in Cortina d'Ampezzo (SC 18 2010) and Nanni Ceschi in Madonna di Campiglio (SAI 2015), Liz Moore in Wengen (DHO 2011), Thomas Pool in Zermatt (SAS 2013), Simon Scrivener in Lech (SC Arlberg 2016), John Ferguson in

Beat Hodler at the 2009 AICC. Photo: Nick Morgan

Kandahar and DHO skiers at the 2011 AICC

Alpbach (AVSC 2017) and most recently Colin Mathews in Méribel in 2018.

Andrzej Kowalski had been the Kandahar's Membership Secretary - arguably the toughest job in any Club - for five years, but also found time to produce a superb results service for Inferno race week. Now he has done the same thing for the AICC. Much hard work, greatly appreciated.

The AICC would not have happened without the support of its sponsors: Highland Spring prominent in the early years, followed more recently by Ski Bartlett, Vallbanc, PT Ski, MPI, Meriski, Ingredients for Cooks, Moose and Coca Cola.

At the second AICC, which like the first was held in Mürren, Beat Hodler made an excellent speech. This excerpt perfectly conveys the ethos of the event.

"What we have in common is a love for skiing and the mountains and an inextinguishable passion for ski-racing. But in the coming together for a team championship there is something additional. It is the sharing of such an adventure, the sharing of our passion with old and new friends - one says in Swiss German 'shared sorrow is a half sorrow and shared fun is double fun'…." wonderful words that epitomise the AICC.

From the outset it was my hope that AICC clubs would host the championship in turn, if they so wished. The international committee is there to oversee and maintain the spirit of the event, tweak rules when required and help with sponsorship which is essential for the host club. The championship has been designed so that bonds can be strengthened between the clubs. Apart from racing, there is plenty of time for free skiing and socialising.

Teams from each ski club compete in a two - run Giant Slalom and a super G, both races equally weighted for the Championship. With several age categories for men and women, each team consists of 3 or 4 skiers, the team's time being the sum of the times

The 2016 AICC was hosted by Simon and Peter Scrivener for the Arlberg Ski Club. Photo: Nigel Fawkes

Parallel Slalom winners, 2014 AICC

of the 3 fastest skiers in each run. In the spirit of this team event, there are no prizes for individual performance.

In addition, the host club is encouraged to run a Parallel Slalom after the other two races, run for fun as a knock-out competition between teams made up of skiers from more than one club, of mixed sex and mixed ability.

Socialising is a key aspect of the AICC and the programme always reflects that. There is a welcome drinks party on the first evening, a "mountainside dinner" after the GS and a prize-giving and gala dinner on the last evening.

The first eleven AICCs have gone well - exceeding all I could have hoped for in terms of great racing, good sportsmanship and conviviality in beautiful Alpine locations. Naturally there have been a few bumps along the way, and some funny moments.

My efforts to enlist clubs from all the AK resorts was successful only in the case of the Arlberg. In Germany, Garmisch SC was not able to take part but for some time I had been aware of a group of German families and friends who regularly visited Mürren to race in the Inferno under the team name of 'Sun Dogs'. I encouraged them to form or become members of a German club and consider participation in the AICC, and my overtures bore fruit in the most unexpected way one January day, when one of the prettier Sun Dogs approached me to declare that she was very interested in the Intercourse Championship. I replied that I liked the way she was thinking: the door to the amateur intercourse championship is always open.

In Lech at the 2016 AICC a group of racing friends took the Rüfikopf cable car to find some late afternoon powder snow. My good friend John Ferguson spotted that I was wearing specs inside my googles, a system which has always worked well for me. He said that I absolutely should try contact lenses and extolled the virtues of them at length to the assembled throng until the cable-car arrived at the top station. At which point he turned around and walked straight into one the cable car's vertical poles. "I'm afraid you're not selling them to me," I said.

About a year after the Duke of Kent presided over the Kandahar AGM, he accepted my invitation to the 2009 Inferno: HRH's first visit to Mürren for almost 50 years. His four-day visit went extremely well and the Duke seemed to enjoy himself, much credit for which lies at the door of his charmingly relaxed and efficient equerry Hamish Barne. Fortunately, an embarrassing muddle that might have resulted from the fact that the Duke and my brother John had identical old and decidedly lived-in ski jackets, didn't.

I tried to make the Duke's time with us as varied and interesting as possible. All main contributors to the Club who were in Mürren at the time had lunch or dinner with him. I hosted four lunch and four dinner parties for our Royal guest and involved more than 50 Kandahar members.

The Duke of Kent skied with many of us and was invited to start the Inferno, which with the snow being good was scheduled to start from the Schilthorn. But the weather turned, and the start had to be moved down to the Allmendhubel. It was fitting that Kurt Huggler, the race's Hon President and architect of the Inferno week we know today, was at the Duke's side for the first Royal start of the Inferno. Racer number 1, defending Inferno champion Mario Teuscher, did not let the excitement of being sent on his way by a member of the Royal family disturb his focus, and won again.

The week certainly had its moments. One of our most friendly members, who had no idea that the Duke of Kent was with us, came up and greeted me warmly one morning. Before moving on he gave HRH a pat on the back and said, "lovely to see you as well!" Somewhat in shock, I burbled an apology to the Duke, who was quite relaxed about it.

Later in the day the friendly member came up to me again, looking rather perplexed, and enquired who it was that he had slapped on the back earlier: he vaguely recognised him, but could not put a name to the face. To give him a clue I suggested Wimbledon; the member still looked blank. "How about the balcony of Buckingham Palace?" I said. A look of horror crossed his face, and a charming apology soon followed.

Over dinner in the Hotel Eiger's dining room, a well-respected member of the Club asked HRH a perfectly reasonable question: "Did you ski race in the Forces?" HRH understood 'Forties' rather than 'Forces' and replied, "how old do you think I am?" It took some time to untangle the crossed wires, but my suggestion that I would visit my unfortunate friend in the Tower set the evening back on an even keel and made HRH chuckle.

My chairmanship ended in 2011, after a fruitful five years during which I had been well supported by the Board and other members of the Kandahar who just wanted to contribute. During my term the membership had grown and, more important, so had the level of sporting activity within the Club. It was also satisfying to know that the Club's reserves had grown by almost £50,000.

Through all my years on the Kandahar board, Bobby Cohen has been a constant. A keen racer as a junior and in his university days, Bobby's working life has been in the law, and he has been a wise source of counsel for a host of Directors and Chairmen. He is precise and meticulous, always has the Club's best interests at heart and if he carries on much longer he will have been involved in the running of the Kandahar for longer than Arnold Lunn. To rephrase Margaret Thatcher's famous remark about Willie Whitelaw, every club needs a Bobby. But who was his wise counsellor when he was Chairman, I wonder?

Annette Hughes is the longest-serving Hon Secretary in the Kandahar's history, and has seen five Chairmen in post. I first met Annette in the 1990s when she was an efficient and friendly Ski Club of Great Britain representative in Mürren. I felt that she would be a breath of fresh air for the Kandahar board and marked her down as a future Hon

Bobby Cohen, destination Sustenhorn, 30th April 2011   **Sir Steve Redgrave in my catsuit for the 2012 Inferno**

Secretary. Bringing her professional IT skills to bear, she made the Club's first website and acted as Kandahar webmaster for many years.

During my term as Chairman I was delighted to welcome Britain's greatest Olympian to the Kandahar and to the Inferno. Sir Steve Redgrave's five Olympic rowing gold medals over a 16-year period is an achievement that is hard to see being equalled let alone beaten. Steve is a good skier and a very competitive curler. When a Kandahar member pipped him to our curling gold in 2013, Sir Steve claimed to be delighted, saying, "I've never won a silver medal before."

Peter Lunn in 2010

In November 2011, five days after my election as Kandahar President at the AGM, we received the sad news that the Club's last Original Member, Peter Lunn, had died at the age of 97. It should not have come as a shock, but it did. I knew Peter wanted to ski at 100 and he was a man of such steely determination, I had always assumed he would.

Peter had a long, high-achieving life: 95 years of skiing that spanned the development of the sport from the Great War to the 21st Century. There is no doubt that our country owes Peter a great debt of gratitude for his national service, the detail and full extent of which remains known to few, as befits Secret Service work. And I am sure that Peter did not receive the recognition he deserved as an international racer because his father was so anxious about accusations of nepotism. Such are the difficulties faced by high-achieving sons of famous fathers.

Aged 8, or possibly 9, Peter took part in an all-ages race with a geschmozzle start. As the older competitors sped off down the slope, an onlooker shouted, "Good Luck, Peter!" Peter executed a smart stem-christiania turn and stop to face the well-wisher, doffed his cap, said "thank you, sir" and proceeded to overhaul the field and win the race. Peter's many other fine results included 12th in the Alpine Combined at the 1936 Winter Olympic Games, when Alpine skiing made its Olympic debut. The Games were held in the shadow of Nazi propaganda, and Peter and his father declined to attend the opening ceremony. "I didn't much like marching around," Peter explained, in his usual understated way. He always said he felt he should have gone faster in the downhill.

Work commitments kept Peter away from the Inferno until his mid-sixties, but he carried on competing in it until 2005, when he was 90. By the time he died he had been a Kandahar member for nearly 88 years.

On election I was the youngest Kandahar President since Antony Knebworth in 1931. That is my cue to pay tribute to one of the most fascinating of the early Kandahar stars. Even when I arrived in Mürren as a youngster, some forty years after Antony's death, the memory of him as the ultimate sporting English gentleman lived on there. In his short life he made a lasting contribution to the Club, and what we think of as the Kandahar spirit, much as Olivia (Liv) Byrom did nearly a century later.

I visited the family home, Knebworth House, in February 2017 and I was pleased to see that there is a glass cupboard on display, dedicated to Antony's love of skiing.

Antony Knebworth

Antony Bulwer-Lytton, Viscount Knebworth, was an all-round sportsman, a gifted writer and a mercurial personality who carried the flag for a generation that lived it large through the Twenties as though there would be no tomorrow. For Antony, there wasn't.

The son of the second Earl of Lytton, Antony was godson to Edward VII and a page boy at the coronation of George V in 1911. From Eton (1916-1922) he moved seamlessly to Oxford and became a leading light of the fashionable winter scene in Mürren.

An original member of the Kandahar, he won the Roberts of Kandahar in 1924 and was a member of the first BUSC (British University Ski Club) team, finishing second to Walter Amstutz in the straight race against the Swiss Academic Ski Club (SAS). He captained the victorious BUSC team in 1928 and the defeated BUSC team of 1929. He captained the Kandahar teams which won the Bernese Oberland Shield - a team competition between Kandahar and Wengen's DHO - in 1928 and 1929.

After a brief spell of stockbroking he decided on politics, moved to Conservative Central Office, contested the Labour stronghold of Shoreditch in the 1929 General Election, and lost. In 1931 he had better luck and was returned as Conservative Member of Parliament for Hitchin. That same year he joined the Auxiliary Air Force and started to train as a pilot, qualifying in 1932. Having 'got his wings', he bought a Moth aeroplane and fatally crashed it the following year, two weeks before his 30th birthday. 'Whom the Gods love, die young' ....

Antony Knebworth

Martha's Meadow

A small corner of Mürren is named after the most famous of the pranks for which
Antony was notorious. This one played out in January 1924, and here is his account
of it, as written in a letter to his mother in February of that year.

*'There is a ladies' race at Mürren for a cup given by Lady Denman, and I thought it would be
such fun to dress up and enter as the girl from St. Moritz 'très chic pour le ski', so I entered my
name on the list as Martha Mainwaring, and asked Arnold (Lunn) if he minded.*

*He said No, but eventually, on the evening before the race, seeing a nasty glint in my eye, said I'd
better not! So I got up very late the next morning and met Mrs. Arnold just leaving the hotel. She
said 'oh, Antony, I thought you'd gone back ages ago with the other competitors'. I said Arnold
said I wasn't to, but she said that was rot and that he was expecting me to and thought it was
going to be the most marvellous rag.*

*I hadn't got anything ready at all then, but they dressed me up anyhow in a skirt and jumper and
scarf. The only hair we could get was a beard, which I put over one ear and the hat over the other!
I looked the most poisonous sight, but it was snowing so no one could see very well! I hid behind
a rock half way down the course, and, after the first two had passed me, dashed out and pursued
them and passed them. They were puzzled to death, wondering who this strange lady was, though
with true female eyes they knew they hadn't seen that jumper at the start! All the anxious mothers
waiting for their daughters at the finish were awfully fussed too when this scarecrow arrived first.
It was quite amusing, but unfortunately the lady who was first when I passed them ended up in
second and said I'd put her off, which was quite idiotic, as I passed her 20 yards away and didn't
run on the course at all (it was much too steep and frightening!) but she made the hell of a fuss
all day, so I thought the least I could do was to apologise, which I did, I don't suppose I shall
ever be forgiven!....'*

Antony Knebworth takes off

Arnold Lunn's recollection of how Martha's Meadow - the gentle open slope beneath the Kandahar piste - got its name is slightly different. In "The Bernese Oberland" (1958), disclaiming prior knowledge of the stunt, he wrote:

" *The entry for The Lady Denman Cup …. included a 'Martha Mainwaring', an entry which very much puzzled the organisers …." Martha, when she came into view, "looked grotesque but skied divinely, and passed through the finishing posts an easy winner."*

Lunn was not beyond repetition, and the story reappears, embellished, in "The Kandahar Story" (1969):

"*…. suddenly from behind a rock a dreadful apparition appeared - a rouged and powdered female in wig, jumper and skirt. Suddenly I realised that Martha was none other than Antony. He set off in hot pursuit of Betty Schuster who was put off by this unknown female competitor and lost the race accordingly to Dora Fox. I skied down to the finish, furious with Antony for ragging an important race.*

'Don't you recognise this jumper?' asked Antony.
'No, why the hell should I?' I replied.
Only because it is Mabel's.'
My wife had been privy to the plot …."

Werner Margreiter at the 2017 AICC

The move from Chairman to President involves stepping back. I enjoyed supporting Nick Morgan in his work as Chairman, but I did find it strange to go from a leading role to a supporting one. Nick had a good five years at the helm, his most important achievement perhaps being to negotiate a reciprocity agreement between the Kandahar and the Oriental Club. That gave us a London home again. The arrangement has been of huge benefit to our members and no doubt it adds useful footfall and bar takings at this prestigious London club.

I have already mentioned my boyhood meeting with the great Franz Klammer. I was introduced to him by the only member of the Austrian ski team who spoke English, Werner Margreiter. Our paths crossed again 38 years later when 'Dwina and I along with our friends Nick and Carolyn Morgan were invited to attend the 85th celebrations of the Arlberg Kandahar in St Anton.

Returning to 2013, Nick was keen, as we all were, to view the 'Karl Schranz' piste that had replaced the old AK run, no longer fit for purpose. We were amazed that Werner was able to take us all for an inspection just before the Ladies' World Cup race was due to start. Werner eventually let slip that he had designed the race piste. Through others we later learned that after his distinguished racing career he became a top coach. He managed the highly successful Austrian men's team at the Winter Olympics in Nagano (Japan) in 1998, when the Austrians more or less cleaned up the medals table. In the 1999/2000 season they had a record for World Cup points; no team has come close, before or since.

In January 2016 'Dwina and I hosted Werner Margreiter and his girlfriend Rosita in Mürren, and Nick and Carolyn Morgan joined us. In excellent conditions, skiing with Werner on and off the piste was a great education and tremendous fun. It was a memorable weekend.

Family Palmer, 2018. Photo: © Millie Pilkington

Family favourites

'Dwina and I first skied together in Mürren in the spring of 1994. She was still a novice, but soon picked it up, greatly assisted by my old friend Sam Hulse. Her finest hour on skis came when she won the Ladies British Masters in Courmayeur in February 2002, a terrific achievement. By this time Sophie had skied a few times and Mark was to follow suit the following year. 'Dwina and I count ourselves lucky that both children have developed a great love for skiing.

I did not want them to ski in Mürren until they were fairly accomplished, as it can be a daunting resort for the beginner. After holidays in Courmayeur, Méribel, Cortina d'Ampezzo and Saas Fee, both are now good skiers, blessed with natural balance. Mark raced in the under 11s at the British Ski Championships but does not seem to be motivated by racing at the moment, preferring to have fun in the powder and the jump park, where he is fearless and well-balanced.

Jumping is something I have always been poor at and try to avoid, but Mark loves it. Mürren's jump parks have been a fantastic addition in recent seasons, and he enjoys sharing airtime with Jake Lunn, the son of Bernie and Julia and a hugely talented all-round skier.

Mr and Mrs Palmer

'Dwina, British Masters Champion, 2002

Mark and Sophie. Photo: © Millie Pilkington

Mark loves jumping

Powder day; Louis Tucker took this picture of me near Klosters in 2015

Mark won his first ski race in Klosters in 2009

Sophie has always loved racing

'Dwina in powder on the Schilthorn

Sophie vorlaufing the Inferno in 2013. Photo: Beatrice Gertsch

The children also loved skiing in Klosters, where we went for a New Year holiday in 2009/10, thanks to Johnny Taylor who introduced us to this superb resort. Klosters is home to another great ski club, Marden's, whose members welcomed us to a post-Christmas drinks party and invited the children to participate in the ski races as guests or members. We decided on the latter, and nearly ten years later we are still members of this proud Club.

The races went well for both children. Mark managed to win his giant slalom, so his only skiing victory to date is in Klosters and his name is proudly engraved on the Muraigl Cup for 2009. Four winters later, 'Dwina and I were back in Klosters for the excellently hosted AICC of 2014. The following year Louis Tucker asked me back for a few days of spring skiing that included an off piste day from Klosters to Arosa, finishing close to Lenzerheide. It was a pleasure to revisit these two areas after nearly forty years. The sun shone and the powder snow was perfect.

Sophie is competitive and determined, and she loves the thrill of racing. We were proud parents when she raced as a 16-year-old vorlaufer in the 2013 Inferno. It was cold at the top, around -14C, but the weather was sunny and the race was over the full course. It was a wonderful experience for Sophie and her time of 18 minutes 31 was commendable: at that age there is a lot that can go wrong on the way down, but luckily our daughter is made of tough stuff. She also vorlaufed in the AICC races in Zermatt two months later.

'Dwina loved skiing as soon as she took it up in the early 1990s and rapidly became adept. Breaking her left leg in 8 places while horse riding in September 2006 was a setback, to say the least, but she soon recovered her poise, despite a nervous husband, and enjoys all forms of skiing apart from downhill racing which her surgeon (with my support) has barred her from.

'Dwina racing the Inferno. Photo: Nick Morgan

In 2001 I had decided to present a family cup for the Inferno. This is open to all members of my family, except me .... but I am Chairman of judging. The race result is decided with the addition of some handicapping, and there naturally have to be at least two competitors. My godson and nephew Alexander Davis won in 2001 and 2002, 'Dwina won in 2003 and 2006 and my goddaughter Emily Palmer won in 2011 and 2015.

By the early 2000s, although only in my late thirties, I was beginning to feel the effects of a sporting life. I was forever pulling muscles and in particular suffering from groin strains. Eventually there was no avoiding an operation. That was successful, but it was clear that I needed to stretch more and look after myself better. Regular sports massage has made a massive difference to my sporting performances in the years since my 40th birthday.

The ministrations of three people have kept me going, and I owe a great debt of gratitude to them all. Liza Adams, a Bridport-based osteopath, sorted out a variety of chronic muscular problems just after the Millennium. Tanya Gibbs is an excellent personal trainer and sports therapist who has kept me in some semblance of shape for the last decade, and Celia Cohen's physio skills helped me through a chronic neck problem a couple of years ago. Without them, my ski racing days would have ended far earlier. I must also mention Satpremo in Mürren: he is highly professional and keeps my body in working and skiing order, so that I can carry on enjoying my winter sports. Regular sports massage does not work for everyone, but it has made a huge difference to me over the years. Thank you, Liza, Tanya, Celia and Satpremo.

I'm often asked to recommend ski resorts to friends. This can be tricky because we all have different priorities. The main criteria are normally standard of runs, number of runs, linking of ski areas, off-piste choices, mountain restaurants, village charm, suitability for children, car free or easy-access.

Magical Mürren

Charles Palmer-Tomkinson

Favourite places

Many people love to go to a new ski resort every year. Despite my attachment to Mürren I am also in that camp, and because I ski for a month every year, I normally achieve it. So are here are my top six European resorts, presented with the proviso that I have not skied everywhere in the Alps - nor will I - and the admission that, inevitably, one's impressions are affected by the weather and snow conditions.

Mürren. Where else? It is where I learnt to ski, where we now have a home and so many of our happiest memories. It is one of prettiest resorts in the world - if not the prettiest - with one of the most stunning Alpine panoramas; it is rarely crowded, is high enough to give excellent snow reliability, has great off-piste .... but everywhere has a weakness and Mürren's would be the limited piste skiing.

Klosters and Davos - to my mind one has to stay in Klosters, as Davos is too much like a city. Even Klosters is not that pretty, but the skiing is simply fantastic. Klosters is home of the Marden's Club and the Palmer-Tomkinson family, which has produced a hatful of top-flight ski racers down the generations. Charles P-T skied in the 1964 Olympics and remains a complete and graceful skier, as I discovered fifty years later. His son James runs PT Ski, a Klosters specialist tour operator.

Zermatt - the beauty of the Matterhorn .... an array of fine red and black runs interspersed with excellent mountain restaurants .... great off-piste possibilities. A magical resort.

St Anton, Lech and Zürs - the home of Hannes Schneider, the world's first ski guru. The historical links forged by the Arlberg Kandahar (AK) are still commemorated today, by Kandahar pistes in Chamonix and Garmisch. In addition to the warm hospitality of the Austrian people, the ski area is varied and beautiful, and they have made huge investments in recent years with new lifts and the removal of the railway

Klosters men in Mürren - James Palmer-Tomkinson and Louis Tucker

One of my favourite skiing posters
from one of my favourite resorts

Ski Club Arlberg hosted the 2016 AICC
at Lech

The beautiful Dolomites behind Cortina d'Ampezzo

line from the heart of St Anton. Lech was home to the 2016 AICC which was brilliantly run by brothers Simon and Peter Scrivener - good friends and great skiers. In 2018 they kindly arranged for Nick Morgan, Colin Mathews, Alex Howard and me to become members of the renowned SC Arlberg. It was a great honour for us to be awarded our membership by 1992 Olympic downhill champion Patrick Ortlieb at the AICC in Méribel.

Cortina d'Ampezzo - it's all about the scenery here. The Dolomites are majestic, glowing pink and gold in the evening light - Alpine beauty at its best. The ski areas are tremendous, but a car is a must. This beautiful north-eastern corner of Italy is the home of the 'Via Ferrata', many examples of which were made when the mountains were a battleground in the First World War, with Italian and Austrian troops fighting for several years in appalling conditions. A century later, tranquillity is restored.

The Three Valleys - this huge area has something for everyone. My least favourite valley is Courchevel, which I've often found crowded with skiers going too fast for their skill set. Méribel is my favourite valley, with beautiful chalets on the steep slopes above the town and an array of great skiing. Heading over to the third valley from Tougnète, there can be no more beautiful way to arrive than cruising down the blue piste to St Martin or, when conditions allow, floating down the gentle meadows to the valley floor. At the head of the valley is Val Thorens, much improved recently and Europe's highest resort at 6900 feet.

My favourite powder run .... Schiltgrat to Gimmelwald. Photo: Simon Hulse

Favourite runs

As well as runs I have skied often, I have also chosen some that I have skied on only one occasion that has left a lasting impression. These runs are all tremendous, listed in no particular order of preference, apart from my first choice, which may not come as a complete surprise ....

• The world's longest downhill race track is a true classic. Over its full length, Mürren's Inferno run has every variety of terrain, and on race day the piste is immaculately prepared for the entire 7500-ft descent from Kleine Schilthorn (2790m) to Lauterbrunnen (800m). After the fast Super-G start come long paths that need fitness and concentration, a steep downhill section below the Kanonenrohr, tight bends, uphill sections as well as fast paths in wooded glades. Modern piste preparation and technical skis and boots have made this race far less hellish than it was for the early competitors and even in my early days.

• Staying in Mürren, I go off piste from the top of Schiltgrat (2145m) to Gimmelwald (1367m). The run starts on the high alpine meadows above Schiltalp, passes the bottom of the Gimmeln T-Bar, sweeps down through some glades to a tricky forest path and then comes the reward of two of the most spectacular Alpine meadows - an absolute joy when filled with powder. Watch out for the road at the bottom of the first meadow.

• When participating in the 2015 AICC in Madonna di Campiglio as guests of Sci Accademico Italiano (SAI) I discovered a quite superb black run that was steep, varied, wide and in great condition. Its name is Spinale (2101 - 1524m). It is a collection of steep Alpine meadows linked by S bends. I skied it many times.

• Méribel's finest runs are on Mont Vallon (2952 - 2100m). The runs down from the top are as good as any in the Alps.

• Klosters is a great ski area with any number of fabulous runs. My favourite starts at the top of Madrisa (2602m) and is a wide fast red (no. 9) that turns into black (no.10) in the trees. Three quarters of the way down you find the wonderful Berghaus Erika (1650m) in a beautiful valley just below the hamlet of Schlappin. In spring it is a race to finish lunch before the avalanches come crashing down on the other side of the river from the piste. This can mean that the home run has to be shut.

• While heli-skiing with CMH in the Cariboo and Monashee ranges of British Columbia in the early 1990s, I lost count and soon forgot the names of all the wonderful runs we skied …. except one, in the Monashees, that had no name until I suggested Kandahar, since it reminded Sam Hulse and me in some respects of the Schiltgrat. Our lead guide Dominic Neuhaus (originally from the Bernese Oberland) agreed to the name. I hope to ski the world's first and only Kandahar off-piste run again some day.

• Männlichen run number 3 (2230m - 945m) is always a treat, rolling over lovely Alpine meadows with views across the Grindelwald valley to First. More than three quarters of the way down to Grindelwald Grund, the Jäger Stübli is a great spot for lunch.

• At the fabulous resort of Cortina d'Ampezzo, the run that gave me most enjoyment took us from the Lagazuoi cable car (2752m) down to a horse-tow near Armentarola (1620m), through a hidden valley with a frozen waterfall. Simply majestic.

- Wengen's Lauberhorn downhill (2315m - 1287m), first raced in 1930, is the longest, fastest and most beautiful race on the World Cup circuit, and it presents the racer with every conceivable challenge, most spectacularly the Hundschopf jump. The finishing Haneggschuss is not a straight line any more: modern skis are so rapid, speeds approaching 100mph were being reached before the line was changed. The views are wonderful, not that the World Cup racers have time to notice. The race winner completes the 4.4km course in around two and a half minutes. I suggest you take it more gently.

- As for mountain restaurants, I have many happy memories of great ski lunches all over the Alps, but standards can change from one year to the next and until recently stopping for lunch was not a priority for me. So I am going to confine myself to one pick: my absolute favourite, great at any time of day, with skis or a sledge - the Suppenalp in Mürren. The welcome is always warm, the schnitzel is always good and the Alpenrosentee is always dangerous.

To close this chapter of personal favourites, this picture shows my four favourite medals.

Mürren Ski School

Arnold Lunn

Diamond Devil

SCGB Gold

A Second Golden Age of Skiing?

Dave Ryding, whom I first met when he was a teenager, has always been a hard-working, focused and determined athlete. His years of hard work paid off in 2013 when he became Europa Cup (the level below World Cup) Slalom champion, the first British skier to achieve this. Over the next few seasons he steadily climbed the world rankings in Slalom and by the start of the 2016/17 season he had become a regular top ten performer.

I visited Dave and his team in Wengen after the Slalom in January 2017 and as a fan told him I was confident that a podium position was just around the corner. In fact it was less than 7 days away: having led after the first run in Kitzbühel, he held all the other racers at bay in the second run, apart from the incomparable Marcel Hirscher, the finest technical skier since Stenmark. In response to my message of congratulation, Dave WhatsApp'ed me when it had all sunk in, saying "you picked it!"

This achievement was Great Britain's first runner-up position since Konrad Bartelski's memorable second place in the Val Gardena downhill of 1981. Dave now has 8 top 10 World Cup finishes, one ahead of another Kandahar skier Martin Bell, who achieved 7 top finishes in World Cup downhills a couple of decades earlier.

I still believe that Dave Ryding has a World Cup win in him despite being up against the finest Slalom skier for a generation, Marcel Hirscher, and the mercurial Henrik Kristoffersen who could still become an all-time great.

Presenting Blaise Giezendanner with his Alpha K for Super G, 2017

David Ryding with his team, Ali Morton (L) and Tristan Glasse-Davies (R)

Kandahar's first Olympic Gold - Daniel Yule (2nd from right) in the Swiss slalom team, 2018

Dave Ryding in action

Apart from Ryding's solid Olympic Slalom result of 9th at the 2018 Winter Games, the Kandahar had some fantastic results from skiers not representing Great Britain. Both Blaise Giezendanner (France) and Daniel Yule (Switzerland) trained with the Kandahar as juniors. Blaise came 4th in the Super-G and Daniel came 8th in the Slalom and then won gold in the inaugural team event. Either or both could easily win World Cup races in the next few years. Blaise's mother Sara Blackshaw was a British team racer and has been a Kandahar member since 1971. Daniel Yule's parents are both British, now resident in Switzerland.

A Winter Olympic Games return of 1st, 4th, 8th and 9th is a proud feather in the cap of the Kandahar - the best in the Club's history by a long way. I have often boasted about the high percentage of our members who race at some point each year at an amateur level, and it is fantastic to see the Club also represented at the highest level of the sport. That this success came during my last year as Kandahar President is all the more gratifying.

At long last the governing body for snowsports in the United Kingdom, British Ski and Snowboard (BSS), has made its presence felt as never before. Much of the credit for this is due to BSS Chairman Rory Tapner, formerly a successful international banker. He has attracted new private sector sponsors, which in turn has allowed BSS to employ a performance director at the head of an experienced coaching team. I'm confident that the new team will deliver results, and excited about the future for all elite British winter sports athletes.

At Club level, the Kandahar has a great team in place. Richard Fawkes, Club Captain for more than a decade, has done a great job organising and racing by example, although his RAF career has intervened more often than he would have liked. In 2017 and 2018 his vice-captain Liv Byrom deputised for him at Inferno week and the AICC, and showed herself to be highly capable: bright, well-organised, forward-thinking and a good racer. Her death in June 2018 has robbed the Kandahar of its Captain-in-waiting and the leader of its next generation, with a key role to play in shaping the Club's future. Her loss is a personal tragedy for her family and close friends, and I will miss her hugely.

I observe that in our era, sporting clubs either thrive as the Kandahar has done, or lose members and fall into decline. Few clubs just carry on at a standstill. The Kandahar has been fortunate in that it has been able to renew itself by attracting new members from far and wide and of all ages. As well as participating in Club events, many of them have made good friends and contributed in some way to Kandahar life, in some cases joining the Board of Directors. I have always believed that clubs should be run by a diverse and representative group of members, so as not to give the impression of being controlled by a clique. With the Kandahar this has not happened, and the life of the Club has been richer for it. Long may that continue.

Close as the Kandahar is to my heart, family skiing has been an equally important contributor to my skiing memory bank, from the formative trips with my parents to our recent family holidays in Mürren and elsewhere. 'Dwina and I have had endless fun skiing, racing and enjoying powder slopes around the Alps and it has been lovely to share the fun with our children. May they get as much pleasure out of winter sports as their parents have done, and may the four of us continue to enjoy the mountains together for many years to come.

Global warming and its effect on the Alps is a much-debated topic, but not a new one. In the 1920s and 1930s, whenever there were dry or warm winters in the Alps, copious articles appeared in the leading Alpine publications of the day, and the British Ski Year Book, about climate trends.

Contemporary research seems to suggest a trend towards much warmer summers: by as much as 2 to 4 degrees C warmer than a century ago. This is why the beautiful Alpine glaciers are disappearing at such an alarming rate. But there is some evidence pointing to the winters being marginally colder in the last forty years than the preceding decades. The last item from my photo album was taken on 20th June 2016, when I skied down the Schilthorn in wonderful spring snow. If the beautiful Alpine environment I have been so privileged to enjoy for almost half a century is indeed threatened, memories such as this are all the more precious.

Liv Byrom. Photo: Peter Byrom

Spring powder on the Schilthorn, 20th June, 2016

32 Infernos and counting

YEAR	START NO.	NO. OF COMP.	% FROM WINNER	% FROM CLASS WINNER	MEDAL/ POINTS	DD POINTS	AGG POINTS
1986	1464	1302	42%	42%	Bronze/1	1	1
1987	753	1299	38%	38%	Bronze/1	2	2
1988	529	1169	43%	43%	Bronze/1	3	3
1989	347	1224	48%	48%	Bronze/1	4	4
1990		-					
1991	647	1155	34%	34%	Bronze/1	5	5
1992	288	1173	29%	29%	Silver/2	7	7
1993	264	1305	26%	26%	Silver/2	9	9
1994	309	1357	33%	33%	Bronze/1	10	10
1995	411	1226	21%	21%	Silver/2	12	12
1996	327	1263	21%	21%	Silver/3	15	15
1997	267	1334	25%	25%	Silver/3	18	18
1998	280	1545	19%	17%	Silver/3	21	21
FIRST DIAMOND DEVIL							
1999	341	1482	28%	20%	Silver/3	3	24
2000	328	1416	21%	14%	Silver/3	6	27
2001	314	1497	25%	21%	Silver/3	9	30
2002	343	1565	32%	29%	Silver/3	12	33
2003	349	1561	28%	26%	Silver/3	15	36
2004	342	1599	21%	18%	Silver/3	18	39
2005	287	1486	36%	31%	Bronze/1	19	40
2006	311	1531	18%	16%	Silver/3	22	43
2007	314	1580	31%	26%	Silver/3	25	46
2008	332	1582	25%	20%	Silver/3	28	49
2009	329	1601	15%	14%	Silver/3	31	52
2010	368	1699	21%	19%	Silver/3	34	55
SECOND DIAMOND DEVIL							
2011	338	1696	26%	26%	Silver/3	3	58
2012	364	1554	24%	18%	Silver/3	3	61
2013	506	1644	26%	21%	Silver/3	9	64
2014	494	1708	28%	22%	Silver/3	12	67
2015	572	1657	26%	22%	Silver/3	15	70
2016	433	1683	31%	19%	Silver/3	18	73
2017	631	1672	35%	23%	Silver/3	21	76
2018	655	1705	36%	28%	Silver/3	24	79

Note: 3 points for a silver since 1996

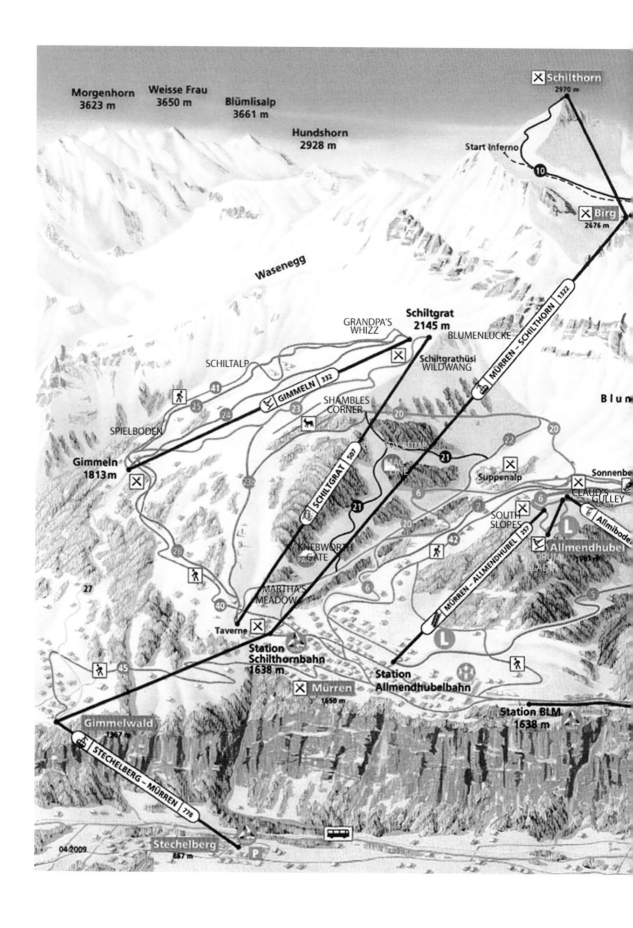

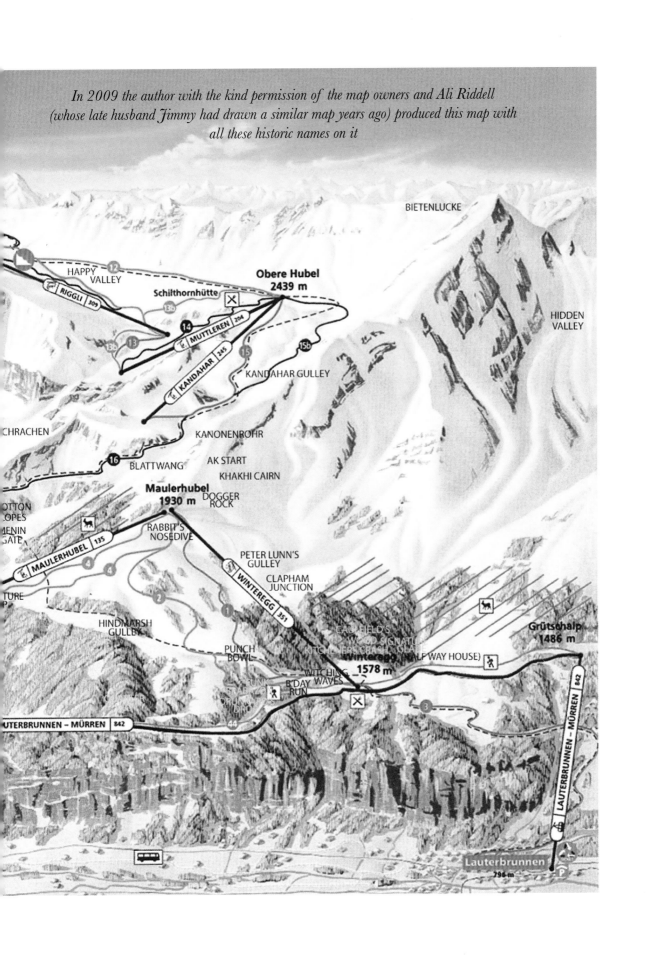

In 2009 the author with the kind permission of the map owners and Ali Riddell (whose late husband Jimmy had drawn a similar map years ago) produced this map with all these historic names on it

I hope you have enjoyed this book. Before putting it down or throwing it away, please consider a donation to my chosen charity, British Ski & Snowboard (Charity Number 1167331) www.bssnf.uk. It will support the next generation of British racers.

I wish you and your family or skiing friends plentiful snow and fun wherever in the world skiing takes you to; always remembering those who were instrumental in creating the sport we love so much.